On th

CALVARY

Published by
The Bible Reading Fellowship
First Floor, Elsfield Hall
15–17 Elsfield Way, Oxford OX2 8FG
ISBN 1 84101 249 1

First published 2002
10 9 8 7 6 5 4 3 2 1 0

Acknowledgments
Unless otherwise stated, scripture quotations are taken from The New Revised
Standard Version of the Bible, Anglicized Edition, copyright © 1989, 1995 by
the Division of Christian Education of the National Council of the Churches of
Christ in the USA, and are used by permission. All rights reserved.

Scripture quotations taken from The Revised Standard Version of the Bible,
copyright © 1946, 1952, 1971 by the Division of Christian Education of the
National Council of the Churches of Christ in the USA, are used by
permission. All rights reserved.

A catalogue record for this book is available from the British Library

Printed and bound in Great Britain by
Bookmarque, Croydon

On the way to

CALVARY

• DAILY BIBLE READINGS FOR LENT AND EASTER •

Hilary
McDOWELL

For Sandra Ferguson, a cherished friend and loyal colleague
whose dedication to the work of the Lord has shown itself in
many steps of creativity and many hours of service to enable
others to walk along his way.

ACKNOWLEDGMENT

Thanks to my sister Dorothy for slaving over a hot computer when mine proved inadequate to produce satisfactory copies on to disk and her own developed more gremlins than a Spielberg film, not to mention the joys of trying to decipher my original handwritten manuscript. Thank you for completing the journey with me.

AUTHOR'S NOTE

This is an imaginative, story-based approach to the events of Lent, Holy Week and Easter, rather than one which sticks tightly to the chronology of the Church calendar. Accordingly, we spend a number of days reflecting on the events of Good Friday (for example), unpacking every aspect of those hours, rather than confining our reflection on those events to Good Friday itself.

CONTENTS

A WORD FROM THE DREAM CARRIER

'Have nothing to do with that innocent man, for today I have suffered a great deal because of a dream about him.'
MATTHEW 27:19

It was approximately thirty years since Quirinius governed Syria and that horrific episode of child-slaughter in Bethlehem by Herod Antipas had given Caesar Augustus a few political headaches. There was still a King Herod ruling in his impenetrable palace on the hill outside Jerusalem, lording it over all, with the local governor, Pilate, satisfactorily installed to keep things ticking over for the Roman establishment.

Judea had never been the most straightforward of regions to control, with its local urban terrorists and malcontents, but this particular year, as the feast of the Passover approached, those in power shifted uneasily in their beds at night. Few insomniacs could have been more uneasy than Pilate himself that particular evening. Perhaps that explains why I was somewhat puzzled when the Boss gave me my latest assignment of dream carrying. I mean, it wasn't that it was beyond my capabilities. Depositing dreams are my speciality—Jacob's ladder, Joseph's moon, stars and corn, the wise men's re-routing, to name only a few examples of my best work to date. But, well, the dream wasn't addressed to Pilate at all, but to his wife. 'Ah well,' I thought, 'the Boss knows best', and off I flew to deliver it to the Mrs.

It turned out that she *was* the best choice as a recipient because she actually took note of that dream and reported it, very fully and with style, to her husband the next day. Sadly, if rather predictably, he chose to ignore her warnings, but at least I had done my job! It wasn't the easiest terrestrial task I had been given. It was a real challenge dodging in and out through the milieu of human-engendered electrical impulses that pass for dreams on the blue planet, not to mention the enemy static that constantly interferes with clear reception from the Boss.

Palestine, in that particular period of history, was choc-a-bloc full of Greek dreamers seeking knowledge above all else, Pharisees and Sadducees both imagining opposite notions of what the after-life might or might not be like, and masses of pleasure-seeking fantasies from the ordinary people, not to mention the increasing numbers of merchants and business types flooding that region around Nazareth—all with their own hopes and fears. I blame the increased access that was opened up by the developing Roman road system for encouraging all this traffic. I tell you, trying to negotiate a straight flightpath through all their self-engendered dream sequences at night was no joke.

Anyhow, like it or not, I found myself with a multi-racial, multi-cultural, multi-faith 'soup' of distractions to fly through. It felt more like swimming at times, and all to reach my target dreamer. How on earth the Boss's son had ever touched down in this muddle, I can't imagine. Well, I can really. He had been sent by the Boss himself and my Boss knows how to do these things.

The lad was a man now and, like father, like son, he was taking the place by storm. The strange thing was, he was choosing to hold back on his powers. I mean, it's true that a human metabolism is bound to slow a man down a bit but, well, he was still the Lord, and he could have let fly if he had wanted. Those who know better than me, in the higher celestial territories above, say it was all for the best. Besides, he was obeying his dad, my Boss.

But you're probably wanting to know *why* I was carrying this particular dream, at this particular time, to this particular lady. Before I tell you what happened after the dream, I need to fill you in on the events leading up to that job I had for Pilate's wife.

Let's go back a little. Actually, I think we need to go forward, right forward to the 21st century, because the Boss asked me to carry a challenge to a traveller from that age and bring her back into mine. It wasn't easy, for either of us. Here is what happened.

+

ON THE ROAD AGAIN

It had been many years since the road to Bethlehem had led her right into the very stable where the Christ-child lay. That 'fly on the wall' experience had introduced the traveller to a rollercoaster of pain and joy as she encountered the child and committed her whole being to the service of her Lord and Master. Never would she forget the ominous shape of the cross as it superimposed its spectre on that small face in the manger. The eyes were radiant as they shone with light, despite the menacing darkness impinging upon the smiling face gazing up at her.

With difficulty she had learnt how to 'take the baby home' in her heart and mind, knowing with each step of the homeward journey that following in his way would be the most demanding, frustrating and worthwhile challenge she would ever face.

What heavy luggage she had worked long and hard to 'unpack' in her continuing journey through life. Each day was lived sometimes in failure but more often succeeding in the Lord's strength. Daily struggles were no picnic, to say the least. But now she had found a resting place, a point of 'staying' in her life where she had settled and was at relative peace. Oh yes, the bills still arrived with predictable regularity. The needs of family and work changed and fluctuated like the turning seasons and the years seemed to fling themselves around to calendar's end with increasing velocity but, all in all, the traveller had found a staging-post with a strong hook behind the front door which held her knapsack and hiking boots very well. No need to take them down again.

Then, why was this happening? Why now, and why her? The

advertisement lay on her kitchen table on a plain white postcard. It bore no postmark and no stamp was attached. She had been in the hallway when the postman called that morning, and it certainly had not been part of the bundle of assorted circulars and brown envelopes that he had fired through the letterbox.

She read for the tenth time: 'Come to Calvary.' Perhaps it was the name of a local church, she thought. Lots of churches held special events leading up to Easter every year. But she hadn't heard of this one. The annual Lenten Bible study journey was familiar to her. She turned the postcard around and around in her hand, marvelling at the brevity of its message, its lack of address or any details of a church. The visual image of those words transfixed her mind even after she had thrown the card casually into the kitchen drawer.

That night her dreams were shot through with the image of the plain black lettering, embossed upon white. She half-woke, imagining herself taking the old knapsack off its hook and polishing the boots. No, she thought, my travelling days are over, and Calvary would be such a steep climb. She turned over in bed and tried to sleep again. Suddenly a thought jolted her fully awake. 'Walk with me,' it insisted. Could it be him, she thought—the Lord? Surely not; after all, he had been walking alongside her now for longer than she cared to calculate, so it made no sense to imagine that he needed to *ask* her to walk with him.

But then, Easter was about seven weeks away and the coming journey through Lent was already heavily overladen with dreary thoughts of self-denial and self-examination, often getting confused with motivations of dieting for the summer swimming costume and the need to feel 'holy', if only temporarily. But, she wondered, just supposing I could make it a bit easier for the Lord on *his* journey, now wouldn't *that* be really worth doing, worth the climb?

By morning she had convinced herself that she should travel again—leave the relative comfort of home and walk beside her Master to Calvary. Her intentions were to find ways to ease his burden and make his journey a little more palatable for him.

Full of fresh excitement and determination, the traveller set off the following day. In her previous journey to Bethlehem she had made many preparations for the leaving. This time she just went. He had called her, and she left, trusting all to his care.

Ash Wednesday to Saturday

THE BATTLE

TEMPTATIONS IN THE DESERT (ROUND ONE)

Then Jesus was led up by the Spirit into the wilderness to be tempted by the devil. He fasted forty days and forty nights, and afterwards he was famished. The tempter came and said to him, 'If you are the Son of God, command these stones to become loaves of bread.' But he answered, 'It is written, "One does not live by bread alone, but by every word that comes from the mouth of God."'

MATTHEW 4:1–4

Feeling like an experienced traveller on this journey, she travelled light. The knapsack hopped up and down on her back, with little weight to restrain it as she almost jogged towards Jerusalem.

Slowly the terrain had changed. Great stretches of sunflower fields had given way to a rising gradient, and a distant circle of hills gradually crept nearer. She was going 'up' to Jerusalem. She remembered from the Bible how the Gospels mentioned Jesus going 'up' to Jerusalem (Matthew 20:17–18).

Maybe I could carry something up this hill for him, she thought, turning full circle to see where he was. But she was alone. The realization shook her somewhat. 'I thought you invited me to walk with you,' she shouted to the silent hills. The low drone of a passing insect was the only reply. She sat down by the side of the dirt path and waited. All day she waited, and all night too, shivering beneath the flimsy covering she had packed. She had forgotten how Palestinian temperatures could drop at night compared to the heat of the day.

By first light she removed the Bible from her knapsack, grateful to have something to consult. 'Where would he be?' she muttered to herself as she leafed through the well-thumbed pages. 'Where did he go first?' Backwards her fingers flipped—before Holy Week, before even his three years of recorded ministry... Ah, here it is, she thought—the wilderness! He spent forty days in the wilderness.

Now all she had to do was to negotiate her compass and maps and locate the desert. 'Shouldn't be too difficult,' she mused, 'in this country.' Sand, rocks, sand and more sand—now where would he be? By nightfall, huge craggy pinnacles of rock towered above her, pitted with cave-like holes gorged in their sides. This was nothing like Western ideas of a desert. Gratefully she headed for one of the caves to shelter for the night. All through the hours of darkness, strange animal cries punctuated her sleep. Her fitful rest was unsatisfying and she awakened feeling bruised and stiff. A rock bed was no substitute for her Laura Ashley covers. Home seemed suddenly so alluring.

The temperature rose steeply through the day, and shelter became more scarce. She knelt by a parched, stubby bush and prayed.

'Dear God, I know your Son is here somewhere, but I don't really think it's good for anyone to stay too long in this terrain. My head feels really dizzy with the heat, and the more dehydrated I become, the less able I am to think straight. Couldn't you just take us both on a little faster? To tell the truth, I wouldn't mind skipping this part of the journey altogether. I don't really need to be here at all, you know. I have a good life at home—well, most of the time. Food is plentiful and my house is a great improvement on your average cave. I only came to apply the benefit of my 21st-century experience to your Son's present predicament. I'd like to minister to his needs, you see. I follow him as best I can, and it really concerns me what he is going through here, so if you could just...'

Stopped in mid-sentence by an unexpected cool breeze across her temples, she opened her eyes to see the outline of a man moving about fifty yards to her right. Covered in the characteristic robes of the nomadic tribesmen of that region, his body slightly stooped, the man pushed forward into a desert wind which had now turned hot and stifling. His hand held part of the clothing across his mouth against the flying dust and grit of the wilderness. She somehow knew it was *him*. It shocked her to see how insignificant he looked against the backdrop of the surrounding terrain.

Quickening her step, she drew alongside him. 'Lord,' she urged, 'please, Lord, slow down a little. We have plenty of time.' His progress continued as before. Without stopping, she removed her flask and held it out to him. 'Have a sip, Master, you must be thirsty.' As he strode onwards, eyes fixed ahead, steps unwavering, she realized that she was unseen. The co-creator of the universe, one with the Father and the Spirit, all-knowing and all-powerful, was, while born on earth, temporarily limited to influence his century as much as she was limited in hers. So she could only observe, not dwell in this century. What a disappointment! She could not help him, then. She fell behind a step, gutted by the realization. Determined to return home, she rested on the ground. Then she remembered the plain card in the kitchen drawer. 'Come to Calvary.' Well, she was on the way, and it must be for a reason, so she would continue.

Looking up in search of the lone figure, her eyes scanned ahead and there, about a hundred yards into the sun, two people seemed to be striding side by side. It was him all right, but now he was not alone. She ran to catch up and paced a little behind, overhearing their conversation. The other man seemed to be trying to help him also. He was holding something out to the Lord and, in a concerned and empathetic tone, urging him to eat. So she wasn't the only one with his concerns at heart, she thought. For a moment she experienced a surge of relief to know that someone from his own time was there to help. But the relief only lasted a brief moment.

As she drew close enough to see clearly against the glare of the sun, she was able to identify what the stranger held in his hand. It was a stone. She wanted to cry out a warning. She longed to grab that stone from the tempter's hand and fling it to the desert floor. She felt the fear of the dark presence of the stranger flood over her soul, threatening to swamp her resolve. The evil one was coaxing Jesus now. 'If you are the Son of God,' he flattered, 'command these stones to become loaves of bread.'

Suddenly it jolted all her annual Lenten fasting into proportion. It made a mockery of her mixed motives—dieting to be able to fit into the summer bikini. Even the sponsored fast at the youth club was beginning to seem more like an excuse for a shindig than what she was experiencing in this desert. Hunger, real hunger, was gnawing at her insides. Exhaustion, dehydration and despair of finding the next meal threatened her survival.

Her befuddled, heat-oppressed brain conjured up images of un-answered needs at home—her life's fears for her family, her job, her health, and the loneliness of modern living, surrounded though she was at home by a myriad of people. In an instant she would have snatched that stone and begged the Lord to let it materialize into the love she longed for, the break from routine she craved, the freedom from her heavy responsibilities... Pulling herself into focus again, she recognized the endless lists of needs and drives and heart's desires that were now flooding her consciousness like harpies, rushing to her destruction. With a giant renewed focus upon her Master just a few feet away, she pushed aside her thoughts in time to hear him say, 'One does not live by bread alone, but by every word that comes from the mouth of God.'

The bad one fell back a step or two as though a physical blow had been dealt. Yet no punch had been thrown. As the two figures moved on together across the parched ground, the traveller sank to her knees, reaching shaky hands out to God in prayer.

Dear Father, are you truly here in my wilderness? Do you really know all my needs? Forgive my sense of despair. Draw close, my creator, and see how your child hungers and thirsts, where no one else can see. The superficial security of a full fridge and a national health service blinds me often and prevents me from bringing my every need to you. Grant me spiritual strength and insight to identify the areas of my life where you require 'fasting' for Lent. Help me to recognize them even when they bear little relation to food and drink. May a renewed trusting, patient, gracious attitude in the absence of my desires' fulfilment be my acknowledgment to you that I am willing to allow you to realign my priorities in life. Help me not to live for mere 'bread' of any definition, but for your deepening life in me. Amen

Thursday

TEMPTATIONS IN THE DESERT (ROUND TWO)

Then the devil took him to the holy city and placed him on the pinnacle of the temple, saying to him, 'If you are the Son of God, throw yourself down; for it is written, "He will command his angels concerning you," and "On their hands they will bear you up, so that you will not dash your foot against a stone."'

Jesus said to him, 'Again it is written, "Do not put the Lord your God to the test."'

MATTHEW 4:5–7

When the traveller arose from prayer, it was hard to tell whether it was the same day or the next. Time itself seemed to have no meaning. Beyond her immediate field of vision, the air seemed to reverberate and tingle and shape-shift into a spectrum of a thousand colours and shades of heat-mirage. There before her, in the evening sunset, stood an incredible city with towers and pinnacles rising heavenwards in shimmering array, a city stretching into the middle distance with a pathway laid temptingly to her feet. The Master and the bad one were gone—or so she thought, until a volley of small stones rattled noisily down a tall flight of steps a short distance to her right. Her eyes traced their source to the top of an impressive building that could be nothing other than an ancient temple. There, balanced precariously on the very topmost point of the pinnacle, was her beloved Lord, with the bad one behind, pressed frighteningly close to his shoulder. The low, conspiratorial tones that the Bad 'Un was using, his mouth positioned close to his victim's ear, were only just audible to the traveller as she strained to hear what was spoken. 'If you are the Son of God, throw yourself down; for it is written, "He will command his angels concerning you; and on their hands they will bear you up, so that you will not dash your foot against a stone."'

The traveller felt such repulsion flow through her that she physically shivered. 'To think,' she said aloud, 'that the Bad 'Un would even quote holy scripture itself in his attempt to trap my Master.' A second shiver in the diminishing light heralded the approach of the cool of the evening and brought afresh to her mind the numerous times when she had cried for an indisputable sign from the Lord amid the mind-numbing, humdrum minutiae of managing shopping trolleys and checkouts and school runs, and setting the video and washing machine and the alarm clock and the… 'Oh, no!' she cried as her Master tottered precariously close to the edge of the pinnacle. 'Don't jump!' she yelled, gasping as the consequences of such a jump occurred to her. She'd seen such nine-day wonders too often in her own century to want to relegate her Master to such a fate. She imagined how television would milk the spectacle for all it could. Shots of many-winged alien beings with beautiful faces, bearing the weight of the man gently to earth as they interrupted his death-defying plunge. Headlines about 'the greatest illusionist the world has ever seen' beamed around the world, followed by a spate of documentaries about every UFO sighting since Roswell and multiple alleged quotes and statements from the subject himself, who would likely be 'unavailable for comment'.

In desperation someone would write a 'do it yourself' manual for budding magicians to explain how the trick was performed—and what about Jesus? 'Oh Lord,' she gasped, but she need not have worried. The Son of the living God was not about to take a short cut in his mission to secure salvation for the world. His words echoed loud and clear, even down to where she was standing. 'Again it is written, "Do not put the Lord your God to the test."'

The shiver turned to a burst of joyful laughter as she released her tension to the night air. Curling her limbs into a tight ball and huddling against one of the walls of the temple, she prepared for sleep, but it was long in coming. She considered how the Bad 'Un had twice now tried to shake her Lord's confidence, questioning his identity and the Father's will. She marvelled at how Jesus had deflected the dangers of self-doubt, not with argument or bravado but with the words of holy scripture itself and with faithful trust in his Father. Her prayers were warm that cold night.

Dear Father, how am I ever going to keep consistent to the example of Jesus in the 21st century? All around I am hedged in by cynical responses to the Bible. Worse than that, more often than not, the responses are non-existent.

Forgive the number of times when I long to take a short-cut in my witness and my living for him. Miracles happen, even in my day, and I thank you for them and for those who fearlessly testify about them. But spectacular signs and wonders for the sheer proof of your power and your will are your prerogative, not mine.

I know you answer prayer, Lord. Thank you for that. Just keep me praying, 'Thy will be done.' Help me to put in a decent day's striving to do that will, every twenty-four hours. I want to be in the right place at the right time, with the right attitude, to help others find their way all that distance to Calvary and on to the empty tomb in your name. Amen

Friday

TEMPTATIONS IN THE DESERT (ROUND THREE)

Again, the devil took him to a very high mountain and showed him all the kingdoms of the world and their splendour; and he said to him, 'All these I will give you, if you will fall down and worship me.' Jesus said to him, 'Away with you, Satan! for it is written, "Worship the Lord your God, and serve only him."' Then the devil left him, and suddenly angels came and waited on him.

MATTHEW 4:8–11

The day dawned, revealing a sunrise that only a Middle Eastern land can promise. As it slowly began to spread its light-streaked fingers of hope across the sky, she raised her eyes to the rocky crags towering high above her head. The city was no longer in evidence and she wondered how much of it had been real and how much a mirage. The outlines of the Master and his evil stalker, however, were real enough. She could see them steadily climbing the highest of the wilderness mountains in her view. A great impulse seized her. She would climb it too! It was easily within reach, and the early morning still held its life-giving coolness.

Climbing hand over hand, the rocks and gullies of the ascent took her weight until, breathless and flushed with success, she stood surveying the incredible view from the summit. It was breathtaking and she was completely mesmerized as, turning her head slowly to sweep its full panorama, she was astounded at the depth of distance and variety of scenery. Before her the great expanse of the wilderness seemed so small in comparison to the towns and cities huddled in the middle distance, and further away stood layer upon layer of habitats of gold and lakes of silver, glistening bright against a thousand skies. This could not be one country, she thought, and indeed, even as the thought faded, the scenery changed and changed again, twice, a dozen times and more until the whole earth seemed to have paraded in front of her wondering eyes. Wealth and governments, business and commerce, artisans' skills and the beauty of a million creations of music, poetry and art. All that humankind and nature could offer lay beneath her gaze, and people, lots of people. She glanced at the Master's earnest face as he surveyed the scene. How his heart must go out to those millions of people, she thought, 'huddled masses' going about their business, ignorant of the drama unfolding in the wilderness of Qumran.

Her heart warmed in gratitude to think how much he would soon be prepared to sacrifice at Calvary to save the least of humanity. Then, realizing she might bear the title of 'least' herself, she shook off the day-dream and concentrated on the conversation now taking place between Jesus and the Bad 'Un. The devil was sweeping his hand in a wide arch and speaking in a magnanimous tone. 'All these,' he said, 'I will give you, if you will fall down and worship me.'

'Hey, just a minute,' she wanted to shout, 'you don't own any of this. It's not yours to give. Only the creator can lay claim of ownership upon the earth.' The words rose to her lips in waves of indignation but were never spoken. She knew no one would hear her, and she wished fervently that she could be seen. The Lord's response to the devil's offer allayed her fears. 'Away with you, Satan,' he commanded, 'for it is written, "Worship the Lord your God, and serve only him."' She almost applauded. Again the Master had pinpointed the problem by way of scripture. Such arrogance and deceit from the Bad 'Un had not gone unmasked. How did he ever imagine that he could steal worship from the Father? Or convince God's Son to doubt the perfection and supremacy of the Father's will?

Climbing down the mountain in torturous, hesitating steps, as the day drew on and the heat increased, gave the traveller plenty of opportunity to think. 'If the evil one could try to deceive Jesus, whose obedience to God was unflinching even to death, how much more would he try to attack and undermine the confidence of every well-intentioned soul on their journey to Calvary?' The Lenten journey meant that it was her responsibility as much to recognize temptation as to resist it. In fact, it would be hard to do the second without the first. Yet she wondered how many folk 'on their way to Calvary' this year even gave the topic a second thought. In her century a universe of opportunities beckoned—goods, holidays, luxury items and all that a consumer society could desire, with credit cards and loans just begging to be handled. 'See, all this could be yours' was whispered in a million ears a day and shouted from advertising hoardings by the minute. What assistance the Bad 'Un had at his disposal. No wonder he rarely needed to appear in the flesh any more.

Exhausted, she stumbled the final yards to the foot of the mountain in time to see the Master also bent double, hands on knees, breathless and exhausted. His stalker was nowhere to be seen and she released a sigh of relief at his absence. The air was fluctuating strangely, sometimes clear and now misty again as though it was filled with a multitude of insects that changed its consistency and transformed it into a living entity. She screwed up her eyes to understand better what she was seeing. The air grew more dense, yet it remained pure for breathing. Soon she could not see the Lord but she *felt* as though he was no longer alone—just as she had sometimes 'felt' the presence of someone staring at the back of her own head, without knowing how she knew. He was indeed surrounded by ministering angels, but she would never see their faces or forms until heaven.

Move on, she thought to herself. You have no right to eavesdrop on this.

Dear Father, how you care! Thank you for taking me through my wilderness in safety. It was rough beyond measure. Every loss, a heartbreak that threatened to destroy. Every temptation, a setback threatening my confidence in you. Every longing, a stinging pain of need unfulfilled.

Help me to walk as Jesus walked—exhausted but not destroyed, frustrated but not deserted, dead to self but alive to you.

In the struggles of the journey, write your word upon my lips and in my heart, that every desert path may end in joy. Amen

Saturday

VICTORY OVER TEMPTATION

Finally, be strong in the Lord and in the strength of his power. Put on the whole armour of God, that you may be able to stand against the wiles of the devil. For we are not contending against flesh and blood, but against the principalities, against the powers, against the world rulers of this present darkness, against the spiritual hosts of darkness in the heavenly places. Therefore take the whole armour of God, that you may be able to withstand in the evil day, and having done all, to stand. Stand therefore, having girded your loins with truth.

EPHESIANS 6:10–14 (RSV)

She had always known life was a journey—that is why she thought of herself as 'the traveller'—but, resting after the wilderness experience, life's journey took on a whole new meaning. No longer did it appear in her mind as a cross-country hike but she visualized instead a journey through occupied territory. Underfoot, landmines awaited to be dismantled, snipers lurked behind bushes and the 'front line' might be just around the next bend.

Laughter came to her aid. It was good to laugh at herself. She was beginning to sound like a general from World War II. Surely, if there really was a war on and Satan, in all his deceitfulness, was the enemy, then God would not leave his foot soldiers without the wherewithal to fight back.

Armour, that's what I need, she thought. I've got to get the proper armour for battle.

Her knapsack was a great deal lighter than when she had first travelled to encounter the Christ-child in Bethlehem, but it was not without her life-support system. The necessities were there—food and water, one change of clothing (not forgetting undies), strong walking shoes... oh, and a Bible. A nearby rock gave her shelter as she propped herself into a comfortable position and took out the book.

She tried to imagine foot soldiers on a Lenten journey. What would they need? Remembering Paul's vivid imaginative use of metaphor, she turned to his letter to the Ephesians. 'Be strong...' he wrote. Well, she'd seen plenty of strength on the earth. Far beyond the strongman's act in the circus, she had watched the unbending determination of the prejudiced and stubborn, the immovable doggedness of those in fear of change. She'd seen the domination of an obsessive parent with a child in bondage, the vice-like grip of a strong habit in control of its weak owner. To counteract such terrestrial strengths and the power of the enemy to exploit them for his own negative agenda would take a strength rooted in a very different source—the strength of the living God working together with a life willingly surrendered to him.

When Paul says, 'Be strong...' he also says, '...in the Lord and in the strength of his might'. She looked up from the book at the disappearing figure of Jesus as he strode in the direction of the desert's end. She could see that his forty days were over, and she knew that to stay abreast of the Lenten journey she must go with him every step of the way.

On her feet again, in pursuit of the Lord, she marched like a soldier does, chanting in time with her steps. She began reciting Paul's admonitions to keep the armour intact. 'Loins girded with the truth, truth, truth,' she chanted to the beat of her every step upon the hard, parched ground. Not a terribly salubrious part of the body, the loins, she thought—a bit too similar in connotation with bowels, if you ask me. Polite conversation needn't go there upon most normal social occasions. Glancing round the isolation of that secluded spot, though, she feared no embarrassing interruption. A passing vulture swooped low and left her with a squawk of disgust. No, she'd definitely be safe in this solitude.

Now if it had been an *Old* Testament vulture, she mused, he would not have turned a hair—sorry, feather—at the mention of such 'innards'.

Bowels, after all, were considered in those days to be the seat of the emotions. 'Mind you, I can't imagine they will ever replace the heart on Valentine cards,' she chuckled. Paul must have had in mind the dangerous and unpredictable territory of emotional life with all its traumas, relationship problems, love-making, anger, heartbreak and domestic responsibility. Where better to apply the armour of truth and honesty than here? Healed family bonds, improved communication and understanding, skills of empathy to put ourselves in another person's place, all require truth, she realized, especially when all that we understand as 'truth' is first based upon the truth of the gospel of Jesus Christ. It is this truth that sets us free from fear in such a volatile area of our lives. Jesus' own words echoed in her head: 'If the Son makes you free, you will be free indeed' (John 8:36). Paul may have been speaking of theological truth, but the body part he chose in metaphor roots us firmly to our daily emotional concerns. The traveller's step was somewhat more jaunty at the thought of wearing this particular piece of armour.

Dear Father, it's easy to be resolute and determined and disciplined against the obvious and blatant members of the 'seven deadly sins' brigade—well, most of the time. But feelings—well, they are kind of 'normal', don't you think, and they stick to a person in the course of a routine day's basic survival upon this planet. Like burrs, as you squeeze and fling yourself through the bushes of 21st-century urban jungle living, they kind of 'stick' to you.

What's that you say, Lord? Maybe I'd be better coming a different route through the jungle and avoiding the bushes with the burrs. Well, I'll do my best, but if there's no option would you help me do a bit of 'de-burring' now and then, Lord? I'll try not to protest too much when it hurts as you tug them from my hair! Amen

---

THE ARMOUR

Sunday

CHEST AND FEET PROTECTION

Stand therefore, having girded your loins with truth, and having put on the breastplate of righteousness, and having shod your feet with the equipment of the gospel of peace.

EPHESIANS 6:14–15 (RSV)

How beautiful upon the mountains are the feet of the messenger who announces peace, who brings good news, who announces salvation, who says to Zion, 'Your God reigns.'

ISAIAH 52:7

It wasn't long in her march before negative thoughts began to slow her steps again. Now where, she thought, is the most likely part of the body to sustain an injury? I mean, what would be the easiest target for the arrows of an advancing enemy? The torso is certainly the largest area and therefore presents a better chance for a direct hit. Even at some distance, an arrow straight to the heart would be pretty devastating. No wonder Paul recommended a strong breastplate of righteousness. Whatever else they will say about Jesus, she thought, no one can accuse him of evil, since he is without sin. Mind you, she knew that lots of folk would accuse him falsely, later in the journey, but in truth he was righteous in everything.

To be right in our dealings with God, replacing sinful mistakes quickly with repentance and forgiveness, covers a huge area of potential vulnerability to Satan's snares. She knew that the breastplate was no optional extra.

It was at this point that her feet let her down. Well, she had been trudging for some time across rough, arid terrain. Ironic, wasn't it, that her chant had reached the 'feet shod with the equipment of the gospel of peace' bit in Paul's letter. She slumped upon a grassy mound, glad to have reached a point where desert scenery was gradually giving way to more lush vegetation.

She examined her toes carefully, moving her hand slowly up underneath the soles of her feet, and paused where a small toughened lump threatened to become a nuisance. 'That's all I need,' she moaned. 'How am I going to see this journey through with corns, or worse?' She instantly regretted packing only one pair of footwear, but then, hadn't she learnt to travel light? Wasn't her Master's teaching training her to rely upon his faithfulness to keep his promises from scripture? Wasn't he supplying all her needs? What's footwear for weary soldiers if it isn't the peace of God in heart and mind, to trust him for every necessary piece of equipment for the journey? Peace is a pretty valuable item of equipment, she thought. But if peace was recommended by Paul as footwear, then she must take steps, quite literally, to walk in the paths of peace. Peace must be an active choice as much as a state of mind. The temptation to be at odds with all and sundry must be fought, step by painful step.

Resting a while, she turned her eyes from the glare of the sun and dozed a little. In a daydream's haze, she let memory parade before her the number of times when her 'unshod feet' had stumbled into conflict. The curt word of self-defence that attacked another's self-esteem. The frustrated rebuff to a loved one's need. The impatient retort that flung word-weapons of fire instead of soothing words of peace and love that might have reached a new level of understanding, an understanding to heal a conflict situation.

Did the Bad 'Un really have the power to effect so much pain and violence upon the earth? She suspected that he chiefly capitalized upon human pride to do his work for him, jumping about from one side of an argument to the other with equal eager glee. He wouldn't care who won, she knew, just as long as humans were at odds. Families, societies, nations would all be grist to his mill. From Jerusalem to Belfast, from the hills of Eastern Europe to the city streets of the UK, all fighting reduced potential spiritual soldiers of Christ to barefoot infantry, vulnerable to attack.

She rubbed her chafed toes and gently replaced the hiking boots, praying as the tightening of the laces squeezed her feet into captivity again.

Dear Father, peace sounds so gentle and soothing—a resting, a relaxation, an escape. But shoes of peace chafe and produce heat rash. They often bite back, the longer the stride becomes and the steeper the climb.

Help me not to let down my guard in this area of spiritual warfare. May I begin to see the clouds of conflict gathering before the temptation to fight back is upon me.

Thank you, Jesus, that those who tolerate tight shoes of peace were called 'the children of God' in your mountain sermon. When the footwear pinches, grant me strength to walk on with you. Amen

Monday

SHIELD OF FAITH

With all of these, take the shield of faith, with which you will be able to quench all the flaming arrows of the evil one.
EPHESIANS 6:16

You will say, 'Branches were broken off so that I might be grafted in.' That is true. They were broken off because of their unbelief, but you stand only through faith. So do not become proud, but stand in awe.
ROMANS 11:19–20

No sooner had she stretched to her full height, letting those boots take the strain as she sprinted forward with enthusiasm to catch up with Jesus, than a stinging pain spiked her right shoulder. Then the same stab in her ankle, another in her hand, and again in the neck. Fast and unrelenting came the pinpoints like red-hot darts, until her brain was racked with doubts. What if she couldn't keep up with the Master? He was out of sight by now. Had she lost him already? What more dangers lay ahead? Was the Father truly guiding her? Time travel or not, could he still see what she was going through in the footsteps of the Son?

Past failures came flooding into her mind, until she felt like a drowning woman. Was she truly forgiven? Had he the power he claimed? Would he really be the victor? Was she called to this journey? Would the loneliness of the trek be her final undoing?

The road twisted sharply around the nape of the hill and she scanned the middle distance for a sight of Jesus. 'I know you're there,' she gasped through clenched teeth, rounding the bend. The wilderness scrubland snagged at her ankles, yet she did not lessen her pace. 'I know you're there!' she shouted as though he could hear her, running blindly, biting back the tears.

From behind, a small sound drew her to a standstill. It was like the gently rhythmic tap of relaxed jogging across the rough ground. She turned around and there, staring past her, his eyes focused on the distant horizon, Jesus came softly, came quickly, came effortlessly along the same path that she had just travelled in such headlong panic.

For a second, as he passed, she thought he was looking at her, smiling, but he kept moving and she picked up the pace again a few steps behind. She spoke to his solidly reassuring back, even thought she knew to expect no reply.

'I'm sorry,' she said, 'I hadn't realized I'd gone ahead of you. I thought I'd lost you. Thought I'd lost my way. Those arrows of doubt, Lord, they nearly stopped me for good. But I knew you were there.' She brushed the hair from her eyes as she ran. 'I couldn't see you but I knew you were there.'

Then the realization struck. Paul was right, faith is the shield to deflect all the arrows of the evil one—faith not in itself, but in God. Of all the defensive pieces of armoury wielded against the Bad 'Un, this is the most mobile, and one of the most versatile. It fits all situations and speeds to each offended part with equal dexterity. Head, chest, limbs, organs, you name it, a shield can protect when wielded with speed and determination. How tragic that it is often the item to be placed on the ground first when the soldier finds herself 'off guard'.

She thought of Jesus' faith. How much faith, she wondered, had been required for a divine being, all-powerful, all-knowing and perfect, to relinquish his authority, his rights, his 'otherness' to the extent of becoming a human entity on a material planet? How much faith had he placed in his Father? How much faith had he placed in the created world? How much faith had he placed in flawed, fickle, sinful humanity? 'Wait!' she shouted as they left the desert far behind them. 'Wait, Lord, don't go any further. Turn back, don't go on. Stop, *stop*, you don't know what you're doing! It's awful up ahead, turn back!' But the Lord kept going. Even if he could have heard her, he would not have stopped, for he did know what he was doing. He was obeying his Father and trusting him regardless of where the road would end. What faith!

Dear Lord, when I am lost in the wilderness of despair or frustration or boredom or doubt, be there for me. When I cannot see you any more in mind or head or soul, strengthen my faith in your ability to see me. Train my arm in the holding of this shield, that the sound of arrows glancing off its strong steel may be music to my ears. No longer may I be a hostage to fear, but make me a victor with you.

When I lose my direction and misjudge the path ahead, please, Lord, step up quickly from behind and redirect my way.

Whatever else deflects my gaze in this crazy, pressurized, violent, tempting, eye-catching world, let me see Jesus. Please God, let me always see Jesus. Amen

Tuesday

HEADGEAR

Take the helmet of salvation…

EPHESIANS 6:17A

Therefore we must pay greater attention to what we have heard, so that we do not drift away from it. For if the message declared through angels was valid, and every transgression or disobedience received a just penalty, how can we escape if we neglect so great a salvation?

HEBREWS 2:1–3

It was midday and the scorching rays of the sun felt like a burning laser on her head. Fleetingly she thought, 'Thank goodness the ozone layer hasn't developed its hole yet, at this juncture in history.' Then she laughed at the somewhat ludicrous nature of the thought. The irony of it made her smile. Here she was, attempting to trace the steps of Jesus to Calvary, to share alongside him, at least to some degree, the horrors of the journey, and she was thinking about a 21st-century threat like skin cancer.

Besides, she thought, wouldn't he know that to be a threat for me in my own time? Wouldn't God recognize her fearful thoughts and wish to deal with them as with all other attacks to her peace of mind? Didn't he care about anything and everything that threatened her walk with him?

She could not expect immunity from the consequences of living in a broken and scarred world, she knew that—nor a guaranteed illness-free life. A head and body left unprotected under the blazing sun must expect cause and effect to take their toll. The real danger would be in not having been warned of the consequences. She knew the danger, so it was up to her to take the appropriate precautions.

How she wished she'd brought a sun hat, and she laughed again as her imagination conjured up numerous visions of outlandish headgear that she'd seen on the TV, displayed at Royal Ascot. Today she would have settled for a kid's baseball cap, or a motor cyclist's helmet. No, that would be too heavy... what about that plastic mixing bowl in her kitchen? She was really enjoying the laughter now, her humour almost stopping her in her tracks as she held tightly to a stitch in her side and jogged, chuckling, onwards.

The niggling ache in her side sobered her thoughts and she began to consider the crazy 'headgear' worn through the ages by those seeking protection and maturity in this world's journey through life. The Greeks had tried novelty and wisdom in an attempt to secure intellectual and spiritual insurance for living (Acts 17:21; 1 Corinthians 1:22), whereas the Jews had continually sought for a sign of God's presence, and their covenant through the years had been firmly based upon the Law, from Moses right to the day of Jesus himself. Even the Lord did not discard such 'headgear' as an aid to right living (Matthew 5:17).

Yet the traveller remembered learning how, in early New Testament times, one of the dangerous heretical sects that had spread like wildfire from Christianity was built upon 'gnosis', or knowledge, the followers believing that knowledge itself could save them. She knew also how religious and zealous Jews had based their hopes so much upon the Law as the vehicle of salvation that they had burdened themselves with a load of extra taboos to the extent of destroying the life that God created them to lead. Jesus had accused the Parisees of just such behaviour (Matthew 23:4, 23).

The traveller was beginning to understand more fully Paul's choice of headgear in his list of spiritual armour. 'Take the helmet of salvation,' he wrote in Ephesians. Only what Jesus would do on the cross could be a means of salvation. Only the proof, in him, of a way from death to life, from guilt to forgiveness, from earth to heaven, from failure at all points of the law to the unconditional love of God's grace, could cover a multitude of sins and pay the ransom to set free prisoners of the soul held captive by the continual legacy of sin.

As that sun blazed down upon her head, she was no longer thinking of sun screen but of the cool, cleansing agent of salvation to be the balm of her thoughts and the protection of her mind in a 21st-century wilderness racked with temptations and doubt. She was beginning no longer to resent the fact that the path to Calvary led through the wilderness.

Without the burning heat, how would she ever have recognized the need for protection? Without witnessing the attacks of the evil one, how might she ever have been alerted to the need for armour? Without the example of Jesus in his courageous battle with Satan in the desert, how would she have fully appreciated the power and authority of the Bible to combat the worst attacks to the soul?

Dear Father, spiritual warfare is a really deadly enterprise. As your foot-soldier, prepare me in every part of life, so that I may be no deserter when I find myself on the front line of battle.

May I train now to exercise my spiritual armour in every part, that I may be equipped and ready in the heat of conflict to stand unafraid and totally reliant upon you. It is so easy Lord, to ignore the need for protection. Life brings many demands, and some days it's all I can do just to struggle to the end of the day in one piece, never mind considering the state of my soul. But, Lord, from your journey to Calvary I see that if you were not immune to attack yourself, how can I even contemplate entering any new day without first buckling up the armour freely available to me by your gracious provision?

About this 'getting dressed' business, Lord, I will need help with that. Satan tries to trick me into dreading the procedure, making me imagine it to be time-consuming and the items to wear cumbersome. I know it's not so, really I do, for you never ask me to carry more than I can bear, but give me joy in the dressing and a sense of humour. More 'Ascot' than 'Pharisee', please, Lord, then we can chuckle together as I march. Amen

Wednesday

TAKING THE OFFENSIVE

...and the sword of the Spirit, which is the word of God.
EPHESIANS 6:17B

Indeed, the word of God is living and active, sharper than any two-edged sword, piercing until it divides soul from spirit, joints from marrow; it is able to judge the thoughts and intentions of the heart. And before him no creature is hidden, but all are naked and laid bare to the eyes of the one to whom we must render an account.
HEBREWS 4:12–13

Wielding a sword was not the traveller's idea of a day out. When she sat down for her packed lunch below a shady outcrop of rock, the Bible in her hand felt somewhat heavier than usual. Placing it carefully where no dirt could soil its pages, she began to unpack the food she had sealed in modern containers before leaving home, glad of the luxury of a square meal—a luxury, she reminded herself, that Jesus had not enjoyed until the forty days had passed.

As she munched with relish, her thoughts returned to the 'sword' lying beside her upon the dry rock. So innocuous it looked, its smooth black cover glistening in the sunlight. Inside, she knew, the pages were well-thumbed and comfortingly familiar, through many years of discipleship living. Like a pair of old slippers, she wore it with ease, losing herself often in its parables, inspired by its tales of great deeds, clutching the promises of God to her heart, sometimes quite literally, as she pressed the book to herself, sobbing on the worst of days.

Now, having witnessed at close quarters the power of God's word to defuse the attacks of the evil one, she began to see why Paul had called it 'the sword of the Spirit'. It alone, of all the pieces of armour he mentioned, was as much offensive as defensive. Here was not merely a book of words but *the* word of the living God, recorded faithfully through many centuries by his servants.

She came from a century obsessed with words. Written media, TV, radio, the worldwide web, bombarded citizens daily with a torrent of words and visual images of fact and fiction, truth and lies, adverts and documentaries, soap operas and educational programmes, all spewing out a continual fountain of knowledge to be assimilated or ignored as each observer would choose. Was her world becoming more blazé in an attempt at self-preservation? With listeners no longer inclined or able to exert the effort to screen out the harmful from the merely banal, did all 'words' now flow before them like so much flotsam and jetsam, to be assimilated only when each individual discovered words and images that coincided with their own preconceived ideas and firmly cemented opinions? When truth is no longer considered an absolute, then all words are mere banter, grist to the grinding mill of ignorance.

No wonder a sword was needed—a sharp-edged weapon of truth that, when wielded in faith and love, could cut through hypocrisy, subterfuge and despair. To reach the heart of the matter, the sword of the Spirit could be wielded without fear of wounding head or heart, for its wounds were never for death but for healing. As a surgeon cuts to the centre of the problem to remove the cancerous lump, so was the word of God designed to be a great deal more than a sticking plaster.

She had seen it combat every temptation of the Bad 'Un when skilfully used in the hands of Jesus. He who is 'the Word' from the beginning of time (John 1:1–3) knew the everlasting strength of God's word contained in the Bible to effect change and to remain steadfast for ever (Matthew 24:35). Such a sword could be trusted, yet she knew only too well how often it was left to gather dust on the bookshelves in her own era.

It grieved her how, time and again, marriages had come to grief without redress to its advice, how teenagers had gone astray by disobeying its commands, how hearts had been broken by ignoring its instructions and guidance. By ignoring its teaching, many in her time were left rudderless, like a boat drifting towards the rocks, drawn astray by one seemingly innocuous wave at a time.

'Take control!' she wanted to shout down the centuries to her comrades at home. Take control of the battle in Jesus' name! He has already road-tested the armour. He has proved that it works. Now he endows it to you. Shield your family with it. Mend broken hearts with it. Attack your worst fears with it. Keep the word as your constant companion and delve into its pages like a drowning man grasping at the last hope of rescue. She would fight with it against the Bad 'Un, never yielding until the one who had already won the victory placed the victor's laurel leaves upon her head also (1 John 4:4).

Dear Lord, I'm not so arrogant as to believe I can win through my own strength alone. As a 'foot-soldier', I complain when the boots pinch, when the march seems longer than I'd anticipated, and when the discipline threatens to interfere with my Western-hemisphere, 21st-century concept of 'rights'.

Jesus, what 'right' had Satan to try to dig a hole for you in the wilderness? What 'right' did the sun have to scorch you within inches of your life, or the desert to starve your heart and soul? Thank you for this Lenten journey you have brought me on. Already I'd rather be more challenged, more humble, less threatened by my own inadequacies, more confident that I will be able to help you in your quest to bring in the kingdom.

All those 'rights' I held so dear, I entrust them to your care. If you can discard your divine sovereignty to stoop in our wilderness, then I kneel at your feet in my desert experiences. Amen

Thursday

KEEPING THE LINES OPEN

Pray in the Spirit at all times in every prayer and supplication.
EPHESIANS 6:18A

Rejoice always, pray without ceasing, give thanks in all circumstances;
for this is the will of God in Christ Jesus for you.
1 THESSALONIANS 5:16–18

The wilderness was behind them now. He, striding through a valley that
was becoming more fertile with every hour which passed; she, keeping
close on his tail, hobbling along with less ease, wishing she could go
without the stout boots which had been her protection against the desert
cold at night and scorpions by day. Scanning the ground beneath her feet
as she followed, she didn't think she was acclimatized enough to the alien
terrain to be able to go barefoot. The stubby little bushes were growing more plentiful, and although no greenery stretched very high yet,
nevertheless there was plenty of shade now for snakes and other
unwelcome local wildlife to inhabit. Better not stop, she thought.

That thought had just crossed her mind when he slowed his pace and
stood silent, a few yards ahead, his face raised to the heavens and his body
in an attitude of prayer. Please don't stop now, Lord, she thought. There
is no real shelter here and we'd be vulnerable and exposed to all manner
of 'beasties' of which I know nothing. If only I could warn him, she
agonized; if only he could hear me. The Master remained perfectly still,

immersed, she knew, in deep conversation with his Father. If only I could hear the conversation, she thought, jealous suddenly of the angels. Was he praying for the world? For what he would face up ahead? For those, like herself, who trod the earth with cramped toes, frightened of unknown dangers all around?

Oh well, she thought, while he is distracted in prayer maybe I can keep a lookout for encroaching trouble. I may not be able to alter *his* course but I can try to keep an eye open for anything that dares to cross *my* path. The silent hills had receded quite a way into the distance behind them.

The increasing birdsong promised the sight of something more pleasant than the occasional vulture whose rude call had threatened her desert nights. Maybe soon they would come to a wadi. She licked her parched, sunburnt lips and swallowed, fantasizing about the feel of cool, fresh water. Her own canteen was just about empty and she wondered how he felt. It had been some time since the angels' visit.

Slowly, without breaking step, she began to circle his stationary form. His strong arms were outstretched now in relaxed surrender and a small smile was playfully coming and going upon his lips. If only she could eavesdrop. She longed to be a party to his perfect communion with the Father and yet she felt guilty at the wish to trespass on something so precious, so holy.

It was this thought that drove her to her knees, and before she knew it, she too was praying. Amazingly she found herself praying for him. She knew what lay ahead of her Lord. Beginning to pray with tears of love and compassion, she begged God to make it easier for him. To discipline the disciples and make them more faithful. To redirect his path through less hostile territory. To open people's eyes to who he really was. To deliver warnings about Judas *before* it was too late, to alert the disciples to Judas' treachery. To open Peter's eyes to his own burly arrogance, the eyes of Thomas to his lack of faith, the heart of Mary Magdalene to the Lord's unfailing love.

Her prayers intensified until they flowed effortlessly from prayer to thoughts and from thoughts to prayer until there was no division between the two, until just to think of someone she loved in the presence of the living Lord became a prayer in itself.

Yes, Paul was right to admonish people to pray not only for the sake of those for whom we pray but also for our own sake. It is when we pray for others that we most feel the growth of God's compassion and love develop within us.

She realized that the Lenten journey is not all self-examination and self-denial. It is rooted in one of the greatest privileges afforded to humanity—the ability to be concerned about the welfare of others and to stand in their place in supplication to God. When they cannot reach out to God, we must do it in their name. When they have no understanding of his saving work upon this earth or have no recognition that it can affect them, we have been given the privilege to plead on their behalf, that one day they may find Christ for themselves. When they are hurting or ill or in trouble and know nothing about the help that can come from God, we must pray for their healing as fervently as they might pray if only they recognized his sovereignty and love.

She wondered for whom Christ was praying right now. Was it for his future disciples? Remembering how he hadn't chosen them without much prayer (Luke 6:12–13), she regretted the number of times when she had allowed a telephone call, a chore, a daydream to distract her from her time of intercession. To stand on the front line and fight spiritually beside Jesus with every piece of armour in place, but without prayer, is like being a soldier who polishes his armour but, when he wears it, has no strength to carry the weight. A Lenten journey without batteries fully charged will peter out long before Easter. She stayed a long time beside the Master in prayer.

Dear Lord, why do I think I have to pursue you in prayer? Thank you that you are here, right here, beside me now. There is so much I need to talk of, I don't know where to start. Please start for me, Lord. Arms outstretched, head raised to the Father, whisper my name to heaven, Lord, that I may feel your breath upon my soul; that I may breathe my day into your hands, and never snatch it back again; that I may hold my loved ones between the fingers of my thoughts, heavy laden with my fears for them, and turn their faces to your touch; that I may pray until thought and prayer become one and I too raise expectant face to the sky. Amen

Friday

'ON GUARD'

To that end keep alert and always persevere in supplication for all the saints. Pray also for me, so that when I speak, a message may be given to me to make known with boldness the mystery of the gospel, for which I am an ambassador in chains. Pray that I may declare it boldly, as I must speak.

EPHESIANS 6:18B–20

'Stay awake!' shouts Paul from his letter to the Ephesians, and just as the thought entered her head she felt herself 'thud' upon the ground, rolling over and over downhill from the impact of an unidentified object colliding with her at some speed from the air.

ENTER THE DREAM CARRIER

I made her jump, the traveller. I didn't mean to, honest I didn't, but I really made her jump. There I was, approaching low out of the sunset, enjoying my flight across the desert and indulging in a few victory rolls just for fun. The flying was easy as I'd offloaded the last consignment of dreams and was really looking forward to a spot of R&R, wave cresting on the Red Sea, when there she was, the traveller, right in my path.

Well you don't expect a 21st-century citizen to be blocking your landing strip near ancient Qumran, and how was I supposed to know she would lift her arms in prayer at the very moment that I descended to land?

I mean, if she hadn't had her eyes shut, maybe it wouldn't have happened, but it did. Crash! We both ended in an unruly heap of struggling arms and legs in the low country edging the wilderness.

I could see that her pride was what I'd bruised most, but that didn't quell her anger. Red-faced and fuming, she dusted herself off and didn't seem at all taken aback to have encountered a low-flying being on her path. I expected to hear her ask, 'Who are you?' or even, 'How can you fly?' But instead she snapped angrily, 'You can *see* me! How can you see me?' Well now, I had every reason to believe that such a question was more *my* right to ask than hers, and since I didn't know the answer anyway, we sat on the sand together and I tried to calm her down. I introduced myself, and explained about dream carrying. No, I explained, I wasn't an angel; and *no*, I protested, I most certainly was *not* one of the Bad 'Un's brigade. Perish the thought! I think I managed to help her understand my bona fide credentials as a servant of the Boss, but she had far too many questions for her own good, if you ask me.

Turning the conversation to her own situation, I patiently listened while she brought me up to speed with her journey thus far.

'It's terrible,' she said, 'the way *he* takes advantage of the Lord. I mean, playing on his hunger and tempting him to break his self-imposed fast by using divine power to change stones to bread. I'm glad I live in a century and a part of the world where lack of food isn't a problem for me.'

She still had anger in her eyes and I spoke gently not to rouse it again. 'You mean, you don't need to be on guard against this temptation?'

She turned her head to study my face. 'What are you trying to say?'

'21st-century Western living has no desires, then? No fiery hot pin-pricks of ambition or daily needs, or relationship gaps?'

'That's not "bread", or any other kind of staple diet, is it?'

'And you've never said, "I can't get through another day without…"? And you've never wished you could make this world suit your needs? And you've never taken steps to manipulate a situation to fit your own agenda, regardless of what "power" you used to do it or the consequences to those whose will would be changed as a result? And you haven't…?'

'Just a minute,' she interrupted with gusto. 'Am I on trial here?'

'No,' I replied, 'but *he* soon will be,' nodding towards the lone figure of the master, now just visible on the path ahead, striding up a distant hill.

'And if you're going to go all the way to Calvary in his footsteps, these questions are as relevant to you as they are to him.'

I left her then, left her staring into the middle distance with a faraway look in her eyes. Instant dematerialization has always been a handy skill and, besides, I was supposed to be on holiday, at the Red Sea.

FOR REFLECTION

For because he himself was tested by what he suffered, he is able to help those who are being tested (Hebrews 2:18).

Saturday

HOMECOMING

Then Jesus, filled with the power of the Spirit, returned to Galilee, and a report about him spread through all the surrounding country. He began to teach in their synagogues and was praised by everyone.

When he came to Nazareth, where he had been brought up, he went to the synagogue on the sabbath day, as was his custom. He stood up to read, and the scroll of the prophet Isaiah was given to him. He unrolled the scroll and found the place where it was written, 'The Spirit of the Lord is upon me, because he has anointed me to bring good news to the poor. He has sent me to proclaim release to the captives and recovery of sight to the blind, to let the oppressed go free, to proclaim the year of the Lord's favour.'

LUKE 4:14–19 (READ ON TO V. 30)

She had always wanted to see Galilee, but not like this. Exhausted and parched with thirst as she was, the long trek from the wilderness had seemed that it would never end. How she had longed, every step of the way, that Jesus would turn and speak with her, give answers to her many questions, hear her as she wished to warn him of impending danger. Yet, although they walked silently, her steps a measured yard behind his, she did not feel alone. For the first time since leaving home, she was able to discern his presence as a living force undergirding each day's task, an energy source that she could neither define nor quantify but that every fibre of her being received gratefully, at the hottest times of the day and on the steepest climbs.

The Master's steps had quickened now and he seemed to tread lightly as though a deadline pressed. If it had been her own century, she might have thought he was out for an exercise run. Then she saw his target up ahead, a synagogue. Somewhat ashamed at her inability to keep track of time, she realized that it must be the sabbath and, of course, Jesus was going to worship. But this was not just any synagogue; this was Nazareth, and after all the rigours of deprivation and temptation, he had come home. It made sense to her, for she would have done the same after suffering trauma, but she was unprepared for what was to come.

As Jesus took centre stage in the position reserved for a visiting teacher and began to speak, she settled comfortably into her surroundings. Aware, as she wandered among the male worshippers who were themselves wandering, chatting, exchanging business tips and fresh news, as is customary at a Jewish service of worship, that if she had been visible to them she would have been required to withdraw immediately to the 'female' section of the building. The Master began reading from the book of the prophet Isaiah, and she bathed in the satisfaction of the approving nods and teeth-clicks and whispered comments of the worshippers.

He was well known in Nazareth, as was his family too. Joseph, his father, was remembered as a respected carpenter and she imagined there would have been many a roof fixed and table mended for this congregation in earlier days by Jesus himself. Carpenters had to turn their hands to most jobs that needed doing. At last, she thought, he is receiving the encouragement and appreciation that he rightly deserves.

Jesus read out the passage of scripture and proclaimed it fulfilled, and a mutter of approval circled the room. After all, their deep faith trusted that God was indeed at work to bring it to pass, some day. She began to feel a little uncomfortable, though. Didn't they know he was speaking about himself? His words were spoken graciously and with authority and their comments to one another acknowledged this, so why was she feeling even more uncomfortable? The voice of a nearby worshipper snapped in her ear, 'Is this not Joseph's son?' Somehow she didn't feel it was meant as a compliment. Suddenly she realized why her unease was growing. She was beginning to recognize this part of Jesus' journey. It wasn't just any synagogue or any date. With full recognition, a stab of fear passed through her when she recollected how the worshippers had turned against him on this day. If only I could remember how the incident ended, she thought.

The congregation was beginning to jostle in an effort to move further forward, to hear more clearly what Jesus was saying. She caught his words, 'Physician, heal yourself,' and realized the irony with which Jesus challenged them to recognize that he already knew what they were wanting to shout at him and how they would taunt him to duplicate works of healing in his own home town, as he had done elsewhere.

She longed to cry out and tell them about Satan's temptations not long before. She longed to open their eyes to how the Bad 'Un was trying to recruit their services, to demoralize Jesus through their petty jealousies. How subtle were the evil one's attacks! How easy it would have been for Jesus to produce a sign or two for the benefit of the sick—people whom he already knew and cared about. After all, wouldn't that be a perfect justification for a miraculous act—to help his own and show them compassion? But Jesus had already shown her, by his reply to Satan in the desert, that the end can never be allowed to justify the means and there can be no short cut to realizing the potential of faith in a seeking worshipper. If they truly believed, this was no way for them to show it.

Sliding between the jostling forms, she tried once more to call to him, 'Don't go outside, Lord. They're trying to start a riot. Don't go beyond the...' But Jesus was already being herded into the open air by a most vocal group who were raising loud protests at his remarks commending Naaman the Syrian officer—a man who'd belonged to the opposite 'side' to those present in the synagogue. How dare he suggest that the enemy should receive favours from God before the chosen people? they thought.

As the crowd, now in an ugly mood, pushed Jesus further and further out of the city to the cliff top, the traveller running breathlessly at his shoulder found that there were tears in her eyes. 'No!' she yelled, in vain. 'Help, somebody, help!'

Where the dream carrier appeared from, she would never know. But there, to the right of Jesus, he stood precariously balanced on the cliff edge with an expression upon his face that could only be described as serene.

'You!' she shouted. 'What right have you to be so calm? Can't you see what's happening here?'

'I can,' he replied in an irritatingly level tone. 'The point is, can you?'

'What?' Her tone was far from calm and her eyes were cemented to the form of Jesus, now tottering on the brink of disaster.

'Trav,' said the messenger, and she barely realized that he had given her a nickname, 'do you really imagine that the co-creator of the universe, the Word from the beginning of time, will have difficulty in dealing with a few selfish, arrogant malcontents?'

As if to demonstrate the point, though she knew it was not for her benefit, the Lord turned to face his would-be murderers and quietly walked back through the crowd to safety.

Stunned by the emotion of the ordeal, she stood staring over the sheer drop to the rocks below, gathering her thoughts through a haze of relief.

'DC,' she said. The dream carrier looked round in surprise.

'What did you call me?'

'Well, if you can shorten "traveller" to "Trav", I'm not worried about calling you "DC".'

He laughed in approval. 'I'm glad to see you've recovered enough to engage your sense of humour. But what do you see in that steep drop to the foot of the cliff?'

The longer she stared downward, the more pictures began to form in her mind—visual images from her own century. The petty jealousies of those in high positions, the power struggles even within holy places, the persecutions of modern-day prophets sent to minister among their own people. The contempt born from familiarity, which blinds all but the seekers of God's face to the truth. No wonder Jesus had said, 'A prophet is not without honour except in his own country and in his own house' (Matthew 13:57).

She thought of Northern Ireland and all the prophets of peace who had been stifled, or hindered, or even stopped from illustrating by their lives what Jesus had just illustrated with his story of the enemy who had as much of God's care, compassion and healing as was considered to be the right and privilege of the 'chosen' few. With what self-styled righteousness had such modern-day prophets been silenced!

The dream carrier still remained at her side and, as if he perceived her thoughts without a word being spoken by herself, he said, 'Trav, you couldn't have stopped Jesus if he had gone over that cliff, but one day you will return home and you can do something where God puts you, to make way for the truth when it is barricaded by these same vices and reactions within your situation.'

She turned to protest her lack of skill, position or opportunity, but he was gone and she had a feeling he wouldn't have heeded her anyway.

Dear Father, am I really put down upon this planet in a particular place, at a specific time, to make a difference to my surroundings? I'm no prophet, priest or king, and as for politics, well, I gladly leave that to the politicians. Yet Jesus did leave the future of the Church in the hands of fishermen and suchlike, and Paul wrote plenty of letters to ordinary people in everyday situations.

When I get home, Lord, only your power can guide me towards the areas of life where I can begin to make my presence felt. Please guide me. Come to think of it, my own church gives me some say, if only I'd find time to voice an opinion—and I'm in and out of schools and marketplaces and entertainment venues and... Sorry Lord, I must stop there, for now I'm beginning to scare myself. Talk to you soon again, Father. Amen

THE DREAMERS

Sunday

SUFFERING SERVANT

He was oppressed, and he was afflicted, yet he did not open his mouth; like a lamb that is led to the slaughter, and like a sheep that before its shearers is silent, so he did not open his mouth. By a perversion of justice he was taken away. Who could have imagined his future? For he was cut off from the land of the living, stricken for the transgression of my people. They made his grave with the wicked and his tomb with the rich, although he had done no violence, and there was no deceit in his mouth.

ISAIAH 53:7–9

She did not catch up with Jesus immediately. The rejection he had received at the hands of the worshippers in the synagogue affected her deeply. Instead she wandered through the streets of his home town, taking in all the sights and sounds of Nazareth. It was a busy market town and people of every nation and occupation, it seemed to her, were crowding the streets. There was much buying and selling going on, children running around doing their chores for parents—some seemed to be slaves at an early age. In fact, whole families of slaves seemed to be out together, gathering in the goods for their masters. It was not difficult to tell the businessmen apart from others, striding along beside camels overloaded with huge burdens or donkeys protesting at weights too heavy in the heat of the day. The sabbath had now passed and religious leaders and priests could be seen mingling with the general populace, distinctive in their holy garments.

None of them know, she thought, none of these people seem to be aware that, just up the road, God's Son has recently been rejected by the very ones who ought to have taken time to know better. How little had changed, she thought, in her time with its business and commerce, science and technology, knowledge and so-called personal freedom. A market stallholder had left out a seat for his lunch break, but it was empty, so she settled herself to open her Bible and turn to where the prophet Isaiah had foreseen Jesus coming in the role of a suffering servant.

She had not reached Calvary yet, but already the wilderness experience and the incident in the synagogue were etching the shadow of the cross along every step of the way. Even though Isaiah was writing about God's servant Israel, the pattern of what Jesus would suffer upon earth resonated through every phrase.

'He was oppressed...' and could we, she wondered, deal in holiness with the 21st-century pressures that inflict so much illness upon so many? In an era when stress has become a disease with the potential to kill many by means of stroke or heart attack or, at very least, minimize our potential to enjoy life on this planet, can we present our timetables and concerns at the foot of the cross to be remade? He who was oppressed knows best how to ease our oppression, if we will allow him.

'He was afflicted...' and she pictured the number of hospital wards she had visited in her lifetime, or housebound people unable to leave their homes because of illness or encroaching age. Worse still were the afflictions of bitterness and hatred in the hearts and minds of those who suffered from the hurt and attacks and wounds received at the hands of our fallen world.

'Yet he opened not his mouth...' He took it all because of the love he felt for each one of us, even to death. She thought of that perfect lamb led to the slaughter in silence, and knew, from the example of his loving sacrifice, that we no longer have to suffer in silence. We are allowed to complain to him because he is a loving God who wishes to heal our wounds and meet our deepest needs. Then we must choose whether to live within a constant attitude of despair or, by his strength renewed daily, to embrace hope, the hope that he died upon the cross to secure for us.

It was not in vain that Jesus suffered, she realized, but to complete the task that his Father had sent him to accomplish. Without the Master's obedience we would still be nailed to our own crosses of struggle, without hope of release in this world or continuing with joy into the next.

She remembered how Paul had dealt with his own suffering by relating it to that of Jesus (Romans 8:18–28). It's not that our own suffering, petty in comparison to Christ's, somehow contributes to his act of salvation on the cross, but, struggling to be his servants in a world broken and marred by sin, we are not immune to its pain and suffering. The privilege is not in the suffering—that's a real chore. The honour is to overcome the suffering by embracing the path through life that Jesus took to Calvary—a path of obedience to the Father, submitting to Jesus as our Master and Saviour and welcoming the power of his Holy Spirit into our lives.

Dear Lord, it hurts to live on this planet, and sometimes the hurts threaten to send us to our grave. I think you know this, in fact I know you do, for you've been here first and escaped none of it, not bereavement or physical torture, not persecution or betrayal from a loved one, not rejection or false accusations, not loneliness or fear, not even death.

My hands reach out to you right now. Grasp them with the love that knows the answer to my need. Tell me what I need to do and give me strength to do it. Raise my eyes from my suffering to yours, that I may know there is a way through every horror.

Let me walk with you, dear Jesus, heeding not the pain until I learn, with every breath I take, to receive life from you and give it beyond myself to others. Amen

Monday

ADAM AND EVE'S DREAM

Then the Lord God said, 'It is not good that the man should be alone; I will make him a helper as his partner.' So out of the ground the Lord God formed every animal of the field and every bird of the air, and brought them to the man to see what he would call them; and whatever the man called every living creature, that was its name. The man gave names to all cattle, and to the birds of the air, and to every animal of the field; but for the man there was not found a helper as his partner. So the Lord God caused a deep sleep to fall upon the man, and he slept; then he took one of his ribs and closed up its place with flesh. And the rib that the Lord God had taken from the man he made into a woman and brought her to the man.

Then the man said, 'This at last is bone of my bones and flesh of my flesh; this one shall be called Woman, for out of Man this one was taken.'

Therefore a man leaves his father and mother and clings to his wife, and they become one flesh.

GENESIS 2:18–24

One minute, she was reading in the marketplace in Nazareth, and the next, DC was carrying her through the air at a tremendous speed.

'Put me down,' she protested. 'You can't just spirit a body away like this, DC. It's not good for a person's nerves, you know, never mind my heart.'

He had to laugh then: her face was serious in the extreme. 'But it's your heart I'm concerned about too, Trav,' he chuckled. 'Look, I have brought you to witness some other people's dreams.'

They were in a garden now, but she had never seen such a tangle of weeds and thorns before. 'Where are we, DC?' she asked. 'Is this Eden?'

'Bless you, no,' he replied, 'but that is Eve all right, over there, shelling peas for lunch. See, on that makeshift bench?'

'So this is where they went after Eden?' said Trav, not expecting an answer, but she received a nod and a sad expression from the dream carrier.

'Well, this is what they did with where they went after Eden,' he sighed.

The woman looked up as Trav walked towards her. She managed a weak but welcoming smile and the traveller realized that she could be seen. Without showing even a hint of surprise at Trav's arrival, the woman began to speak—a waterfall of words that became a raging torrent, pouring out her story without hesitation.

'It's pretty exhausting here on the farm day after day, struggling to make ends meet. Sometimes Adam comes home, grime to the neck, with nothing to show for his efforts except arms stacked full of weeds. But we have a dream, oh yes.

'We will plant a garden some day, a proper one, just like our old home in Eden. There will be wild roses and scented blossoms and fresh green shoots that will grow into strong trees protected from weather and pest. Nothing will wither and die in the midday sun and no animal will prowl around stalking its prey, but all will be in harmony. We will feed every creature by hand as Adam once taught me to do, as he once did, taught by the Maker, and we will pluck the choicest… we will pluck the freshest… we will eat from the…'

Trav felt great compassion for the woman as her voice finally broke down in tears. 'Please forgive me,' sobbed Eve, 'but the memory still hurts. It was perfection, you see, especially at each day's end—that was always the best time for me. Just the two of us walking in the cool of the evening with the Maker. I suppose that's three really, not two, but it felt like we were one. Now it's so lonely. Just the two of us to tend the garden, and hostile animals that need taming, and stubborn soil that needs ploughing, and disobedient sons at each other's throats. I tell you, I've my hands full. When will I ever get time to plant a garden?

'Yet sometimes, as the day lengthens, I catch a glimpse of a shadow now—not up close, but I catch it like a quick dart out the side of my eye and I imagine he's still with us, the Maker. Adam thinks so too, otherwise we'd have died long since, he says. Of course it's hard to convince the boys. Abel listens sometimes with a wistful look on his face, but that Cain, I don't know what I'm going to do with him. Still, maybe when they are grown up a bit, I'll plant that garden.'

The dream carrier drew close to Trav then as her own tears came, and he led her a short distance away to speak with her.

'We all long for Eden, Trav,' he said. 'A place to be safe and happy, somewhere to have our dreams fulfilled and our longings satisfied. The place where the people of the earth have journeyed now includes weeds and wild beasts. Our ancestors forfeited the perfect garden when they disobeyed the creator's instructions. In your century the degradation has developed in all sorts of directions. No wonder they called it "the Fall".'

'Why are you showing me all this?' sobbed Trav, desperately wanting to be free of this tragic tale.

'Because,' replied DC, 'the road to Calvary began here. Adam and Eve did not guess it, of course. In all their pain and shame and fear, they did not foresee how the creator would stand by his creation. How my Boss would speak constantly to Earth through a long line of prophets and kings, and especially by way of a group of people, the Israelites. How, in the end, he would take upon himself the full burden of the consequences of human actions rather than give up on his beloved humanity, sinful though each person continues to be. Having given Adam and Eve freedom of choice, he permitted them to choose to disobey. The Boss is fair that way—he never backtracks on his own rules—but he wasn't going to walk away from his creation and leave it to sink or swim. Instead he dreamt the greatest dream of all. Nothing to do with me, of course; I'm just a servant. God dreams his own dreams. His was an incredible dream of oneness—a perfect reunion between himself and his creation, including all those who had chosen to separate themselves from him by their sin. However, oneness means no barriers, and so the dividing wall of sin had to come down. No man or woman could do this, since the brokenness of the Fall was now endemic within everyone—genetically inherited if you like, spiritually speaking. Only God could do what humanity could not. That's where Jesus takes the task all the way to Calvary, and succeeds.'

Dear Father, I don't deserve what you did for me. Today I want to engage in that journey towards oneness which continues until heaven. First I ask forgiveness for all my sin. Please help me to walk on. Amen

Tuesday

HANNAH'S DREAM

Now this man used to go up year by year from his town to worship and to sacrifice to the Lord of hosts at Shiloh, where the two sons of Eli, Hophni and Phinehas, were priests of the Lord. On the day when Elkanah sacrificed, he would give portions to his wife Peninnah and to all her sons and daughters; but to Hannah he gave a double portion, because he loved her, though the Lord had closed her womb. Her rival used to provoke her severely, to irritate her, because the Lord had closed her womb...

After they had eaten and drunk at Shiloh, Hannah rose and presented herself before the Lord. Now Eli the priest was sitting on the seat beside the doorpost of the temple of the Lord. She was deeply distressed and prayed to the Lord, and wept bitterly. She made this vow: 'O Lord of hosts, if only you will look on the misery of your servant, and remember me, and not forget your servant, but will give to your servant a male child, then I will set him before you as a nazirite until the day of his death. He shall drink neither wine nor intoxicants, and no razor shall touch his head.'

1 SAMUEL 1:3–6, 9–11 (READ WHOLE CHAPTER)

The traveller's next flight with DC brought them both to land in the courtyard of an ancient temple. DC placed his finger to his lips, signalling her to tread quietly to where a woman of Israel was deeply distraught and praying.

'A wonderful and terrible thing will happen for this woman, Trav. It's Hannah,' he whispered.

The traveller looked surprised. 'Yes, I remember, DC, but she has her prayer answered. Her dream of a son comes true, and she gets her baby.' The traveller had read many times, in the Old Testament especially and also in the New, of the intense shame experienced by mothers who were childless or who were not able to produce a son to continue the family line. The scorn piled upon their heads was a real parallel to some of the scorn levelled at Jesus at Calvary. It must have been truly wonderful when the baby was born, she thought.

'Yes,' said DC, as though reading her thoughts, 'wonderful beyond measure, but at a cost. Imagine what it must have felt like to long for something so badly that the longing almost destroyed her, and then to trust God for the fulfilment of that dream, and to receive it, and then to lose it again.'

'But she did not lose it, DC, she gave the baby back to God from her own free choice. She knew that when new life comes, a cost is involved to bring that life to its full potential, and if she trusted God for the dream, she could trust him *with* the dream also.'

DC was smiling and nodding in appreciation of her words. 'You're right, Trav,' he said. 'Now, as you walk to Calvary, can you do the same? What is about to happen to Jesus on that hill will bring new life to all who accept him as Lord of their lives, but at what a cost! Only God's Son could pay that price in full because he was both human and divine, but there is a cost for those who travel in his footsteps. It's not a payment—only he can make that. Salvation is free, but there is a cost of discipleship.'

They were seated in the temple now, and as Hannah had spoken with Eli and then left, it was quiet. DC reached gently to where Trav's small, golden cross hung upon its chain around her neck, and rested it in his fingers. 'It's so pretty, yet it represents scorn and scourging and persecution. It's the symbol of the outcast, Trav, according to the people of this time. As I'm sure you've read in the first chapter of 1 Corinthians and Galatians 3, it speaks of foolishness to some, and even a curse to others. To dream the dream of salvation, to wish desperately for new life in the place of old, we have to be willing to surrender that life back into the hands of the one who makes such a life possible in the first place.'

'I see what you mean, DC. The cross isn't a magic charm to save all and sundry automatically. Without our surrender, God's gift lies rejected, unclaimed, ineffectual for us.'

'Hannah surrendered her most precious possession, the baby she longed for more than anything else in the world. Trav, wouldn't you say that life itself is, to most people, their most precious possession? Yet how many journey to Calvary every Easter unwilling to surrender it fully to Christ?'

Trav slowly rose to her feet and wandered to the door where she could see Hannah in the distance making her way home. She followed the soon-to-be mum a short distance and imagined her dreaming, in faith, of that precious gift from God which would be placed 'on loan' to her. Trav pictured all those in the 21st century who had not yet realized that everything was 'on loan' to them—yes, even life itself. Jobs, bank balance, houses, health, even loved ones cherished and desperately needed, were all 'on loan'. There was only one way to keep them and that was to give them away to God—the only one able to truly possess all that he made from the beginning of time.

The traveller reviewed her own dreams and asked herself, what dream would last or bring real fulfilment that did not come from the Master? She knew that the only answer could be 'None.' She had to count the cost and be willing to give her all for Christ. Like the man building the tower in Luke 14, she would find it a costly business—but God can be trusted to take care of our dreams.

How spontaneously the traveller had grabbed her hiking boots from that hook on her door and set off for Calvary. Great enthusiasm and deep devotion had motivated her journey. Now she knew that the Boss was asking her to consider the cost of following him—the unpopularity, the misunderstanding that might be directed at her, the accusations from those with envy or ignorance or fear within their hearts. Those who did not choose to walk this path would not easily let her walk it in peace. If she continued along his journey, her life would share his sufferings and something of his pain. But would it be worse than the labour pains Hannah would embrace willingly for the new life that would come? Trav realized then that those who try to protect themselves from the cost, or run from it, will never know the joy.

Dear Father, Hannah's dream is a dream for all—to have life, new life within, not literally a human baby but all that you promised and wished for humankind, life abundant. Take my dream, Lord. All that makes life worth the living, I surrender it to you, that it may be made new by your work of re-creation.

Thank you for forgiveness from each sin confessed. Without that, my journey ends in cul-de-sacs of failure. Now strengthen me to count the cost of walking on with you. Give me courage in the worst of days to know that the journey's end is crafted by your loving hands when we walk together unafraid.

When I count the cost and find that I fall short by endless quantities of love, please, Lord, complete the task in me that you began the day I surrendered body, mind, and soul to you. If in any part I still hold back, give me Hannah's dream—to relinquish into your hands that which only you can really own. Amen

Wednesday

DANIEL'S DREAM

Soon Daniel distinguished himself above all the other presidents and satraps because an excellent spirit was in him, and the king planned to appoint him over the whole kingdom. So the presidents and the satraps tried to find grounds for complaint against Daniel in connection with the kingdom. But they could find no grounds for complaint or any corruption, because he was faithful, and no negligence or corruption could be found in him. The men said, 'We shall not find any ground for complaint against this Daniel unless we find it in connection with the law of his God.' ...

'All the presidents of the kingdom, the prefects and the satraps, the counsellors and the governors are agreed that the king should establish an ordinance and enforce an interdict, that whoever prays to anyone, divine or human, for thirty days, except to you, O king, shall be thrown into a den of lions. Now, O king, establish the interdict and sign the document, so that it cannot be changed, according to the law of the Medes and the Persians, which cannot be revoked.' Therefore King Darius signed the document and interdict.

Although Daniel knew that the document had been signed, he continued to go to his house, which had windows in its upper room open toward Jerusalem, and to get down on his knees three times a day to pray to his God and praise him, just as he had done previously.

DANIEL 6:3–5, 7–10

'The Bible is full of dreamers, Trav,' said DC, catching up with her and turning her around. 'Now take Daniel, for example. He was one of many who could actually interpret other people's dreams for them, which is not an occupation to be recommended, as it generally gets the person concerned into a lot of trouble. Anyway, as I was saying, he was a dreamer himself and much is still made of his dreams, even in your century. But not enough is made of the dream that got him thrown into the den of lions.'

She turned puzzled eyes to DC and was taken off guard as he whisked her once more to a different landscape. Now they stood looking up at an ancient house of grandeur and opulence. The top-floor window was open and there she could plainly see a man dressed in the very best of robes, kneeling in prayer.

'The lad has done very well, hasn't he, Trav?' said DC, nodding up towards Daniel, framed as he was in the window, calling aloud to the one true God of Israel. 'I mean, third highest position in the land, now one of the presidents, and King Darius seriously thinking of giving him promotion to number one. He must have had a lot of ambition, that boy—worked hard too, and deserved all his advancement, don't you think?'

Trav nodded in agreement but kept her eyes pinned upon the earnest face of Daniel as he continued in fervent prayer.

'Well, there he is then, Trav, fulfilling his dream.'

She looked at DC for inspiration. 'What do you mean? The man is just praying.'

'Exactly,' continued DC. 'Right now there is a whole crowd of his colleagues, a host of spin doctors and who knows *who* else in power, jealously manipulating the laws of the land to work against Daniel and to forbid him freedom to do the one thing he will not stop doing—communicate with and worship his God.'

'Oh, I see,' said Trav. 'You mean his dream was to…'

'Be faithful to Yahweh, the one true God of Israel and my Boss,' DC said, finishing the sentence for her. 'Daniel sat there faithfully day after day, three times a day, without flinching, until they threw him into the lions' den.'

The traveller stared up at that intelligent face in the window and thought how she was attempting to follow in the footsteps of one who was intent upon walking a similar path—a path of faithfulness to God which would lead Jesus also right into a lions' den, where the sharp teeth of envy and power struggles and pride would pierce an innocent and sinless man.

'How are you at the old lion-taming skills, then, Trav?' grinned DC as he interrupted her thoughts. 'Hey, not so sad, girl, don't look so scared. Remember what happened to Daniel? God shut the lions' mouths, but Daniel still had to spend some time in that den, didn't he? There can be no opting out when God calls his servants to put their trust in him.'

Remembering that Daniel's trust and faithfulness did not end with the lions gave her courage. In fact, his courage had led to the king recognizing the supremacy and truth of the living God of Israel. Rather than destroying the worship of Yahweh, the king had declared it to be the official religion of the land, and a reign of peace had begun in that area where Daniel became free to dream all the dreams God had for him.

'Can the Lord trust you to continue in his footsteps all the way to Calvary, Trav,' came DC's voice quietly beside her, 'no matter what you may meet on the way?'

She thought of her situation back in the 21st century. She thought of the many ways in which her life could deflect a follower from worship or prayer; the countless reasons to 'tone down' a moment of potential witness, to silence a word about the Saviour even as it rose to the lips, or the endless excuses—apparently so rational—to avoid an extra deed of kindness or sacrifice to help those who desperately needed assistance in some practical way to alleviate poverty, sickness or loneliness.

'Trust him, Trav.' DC had her on the wing again. Mid-flight he said, 'Trust the Lord to be there before you in each and every situation. Leave the lions to him; as for you, concentrate on being faithful to his calling no matter what you have to sacrifice in order to remain in his will.'

As they flew on through the night, she not knowing in what direction DC was taking her, she passed the time by calling to mind those whom Jesus would encounter on this earthly journey before Calvary. The lepers and those struggling with blindness or other disabilities, and the families and friends who brought many to Jesus trusting that they could be healed. People unaware of his journey, aware only of his love and the power of the living God working through him. How desperately her own world needed to apply such faith and trust, and how fortunate were 21st-century dwellers to have the hindsight of the victory that was won at Calvary.

Dear Lord, thank you for the evidence of scripture to alert us to the dramatic events of Holy Week. Thank you for over two thousand years of the faithful witness of your Church in all its varied denominations. Thank you for the personal testimonies and courageous lives of your followers through the ages.

Forgive us when, in the face of all the evidence, despite every example of your servants in every era, we nevertheless fail to trust.

I know that there is much work to be done, Lord. The television news bulletins of disaster, violence and plague constantly highlight fresh areas for Christian service and dedication but, to make a difference, teach your Church how to pray until it has Daniel's power to make a difference. Teach us, each one, to trust until every lions' den can be invaded by the Father's will and, in safety, lions can indeed lie down with lambs. Amen

Thursday

JACOB'S DREAM

Jacob left Beer-sheba and went toward Haran. He came to a certain place and stayed there for the night, because the sun had set. Taking one of the stones of the place, he put it under his head and lay down in that place. And he dreamed that there was a ladder set up on the earth, the top of it reaching to heaven; and the angels of God were ascending and descending on it. And the Lord stood beside him and said, 'I am the Lord, the God of Abraham your father and the God of Isaac; the land on which you lie I will give to you and to your offspring; and your offspring shall be like the dust of the earth, and you shall spread abroad to the west and to the east and to the north and to the south; and all the families of the earth shall be blessed in you and in your offspring. Know that I am with you and will keep you wherever you go, and will bring you back to this land; for I will not leave you until I have done what I have promised you.'

GENESIS 28:10–15

Breathless with the long night flight, Trav pleaded with DC to stop for a rest.

'OK,' he agreed obligingly. 'Will this do?'

They seemed to have paused in mid-air and for a moment Trav thought she was hanging precariously with no visible means of support. Then she realized that her feet were, in fact, resting upon a slim horizontal rod of some kind. Looking down in the dim light of dawn, she was just able to discern that there were a number of rods stretching below and above her as far as her eyes were able to see into the distance.

'It's a ladder,' said DC casually. 'Well, to be more precise, it's Jacob's ladder.'

'*What?*' she yelled in consternation, trying desperately to detach herself from the ethereal structure. 'But it's for angels, DC, not for the likes of us.'

'You speak for yourself,' he chuckled. 'Besides, we're only resting here temporarily to let you gatecrash Jacob's dream. It's an actual dream this time and I carried it rather expertly to him, if I remember rightly. He is well and truly asleep, believe me.'

'Are you sure?' she asked nervously, peering down into the grey mist with no desire at all to see anyone.

'I do understand your concern, Trav. He wasn't exactly the most desirable character in the Bible, was he? I mean, hoodwinking his brother Esau to steal his inheritance away, even if it meant deceiving his poor old dad, to name just one of his exploits, but you have to admit that he worked hard most of his life and he certainly knew how to pray. That's what he's doing here on this night, chasing a dream of holiness, thinking God is so far from him. This was the place that changed his life. Well, would *you* expect to encounter God while fast asleep with a stone for a pillow?'

Trav didn't answer that, not after her experience in the wilderness. 'But what's with the ladder, DC?' she queried.

'It's a bridge, Trav, a link between heaven and earth with angels ascending and descending. It's where God can even descend to earth. In Jacob's day this was still quite a revolutionary concept. Oh yes, the Boss could send a message to whomever he wished, whenever he wished, and he frequently did communicate with his chosen people, but the thought of him making the journey down to be on our level, well, that was mind-blowing for poor old Jacob. No wonder he was afraid and decided that this certainly was 'holy ground'. Despite the fact that Jacob would have been well versed in the Hebrew tradition both of culture and religion, and trained from birth to cherish the Jewish covenant handed down from the days of Abraham, it was not until Bethel that he encountered the living God and gladly received the promise, personally conveyed to him in his dream.'

The traveller thought about how God had given Jacob a new start, and new eyes to see how he could receive forgiveness and seek the very gateway to heaven, thanks to God keeping his promises down the generations—right through history, until the time was ripe for Jesus to open a heaven's gate that no one could close, by treading the Calvary road to his death upon the cross and his victory from the empty tomb. If only the people of her century could fully embrace those everlasting promises. The Boss's words to Jacob, 'Behold, I am with you and will keep you wherever you go', sounded so like the words of Jesus after his resurrection, 'I am with you always, to the close of the age' (Matthew 28:20). He was the same God, reinforcing his promises to his children again and again through the length and breadth of scripture. Only now, Jesus himself was the bridge, the linchpin to connect heaven to earth in a way that gave a whole new concept of access to God, even for a scoundrel like Jacob.

If only her world would grasp the wonder of this, she thought: God's presence and power of healing and enabling to release all those in chains—the alcoholic, the drug abuser, the despairing, the depressed, the lonely, the anxious parent and the child without self-esteem; everyone suffering misery and turmoil, including those who know that they have committed great sin and those who foolishly believe they have committed none.

'We don't need a ladder in my time, DC,' she told him. 'God has climbed down to stand where we stand, to bleed as we bleed, to rise as we could never have hoped to rise if he had not conquered the power of death and sin and risen before us.'

The ladder was wobbling now beneath her feet at her outburst of excitement, and she grabbed hold of DC's arms to steady herself. He laughed in unison with her joy. 'Steady on, Trav, this ladder has to hold a lot of feet before this night is through. Don't you go breaking it now.' She looked upwards then, with a wistful gaze to where the ladder stretched into infinity. 'Not yet, Trav,' he said, 'you haven't been to Calvary yet. You must finish your journey.'

Dear heavenly Father, how patient you have been with us all. Through countless centuries you have nurtured your children, leading us through wilderness after wilderness of our own making; forgiving those who genuinely repent and ask forgiveness; turning a blind eye when you get blamed for all the shortcomings of the world, even though you are the cause of no bad or evil thing; lifting us up when we fall into pits of sin or despair; and all the while planning for our greater good.

Father, I ask forgiveness now for.........

Lord, I identify all those times when I have blamed you in the past and I cast those accusations from me.........

Dear God, magnify my thankfulness for all the times you have rescued me from trouble and help me to remember them now.........

Father, I bring to you my present concern that, once again, I may know your rescue......... in Jesus name. Amen

Friday

MOSES' DREAM

Moses was keeping the flock of his father-in-law Jethro, the priest of Midian; he led his flock beyond the wilderness, and came to Horeb, the mountain of God. There the angel of the Lord appeared to him in a flame of fire out of a bush; he looked, and the bush was blazing, yet it was not consumed. Then Moses said, 'I must turn aside and look at this great sight, and see why the bush is not burned up.' When the Lord saw that he had turned aside to see, God called to him out of the bush, 'Moses, Moses!' And he said, 'Here I am.' Then he said, 'Come no closer! Remove the sandals from your feet, for the place on which you are standing is holy ground.' He said further, 'I am the God of your father, the God of Abraham, the God of Isaac, and the God of Jacob.' And Moses hid his face, for he was afraid to look at God…

Afterward Moses and Aaron went to Pharaoh and said, 'Thus says the Lord, the God of Israel, "Let my people go, so that they may celebrate a festival to me in the wilderness."'

EXODUS 3:1–6; 5:1

The traveller and the dream carrier rested from their headlong flight through history by coming to a standstill on the slopes of Mount Horeb. 'This is a good place to catch our breath, Trav,' said DC, showing her the surrounding terrain lying peaceful in the sun with only the quiet grazing of sheep to disturb the stillness. 'Every traveller needs time out to gather their wits about them and hear God speak.'

She sat upon the grass, relaxing, her hands brushing aimlessly over the tops of the tufts of moss as she considered her present location. Horeb, she remembered, was considered to be a holy mountain in Bible days. Wasn't it the mountain where Moses saw the... 'Hey!' she cried out, springing to her feet. 'You wouldn't, DC... you would not have brought me here to witness God's call to Moses from the burning bush?' The dream carrier merely smiled up at her patiently, and she knew that he would... and he had. Slowly he began to explain to her that she would not see the bush, as that was for the eyes of Moses only. 'But look,' he continued, 'see that lone shepherd down there, on his knees? He looks as though he is talking to thin air, but he's not.'

Moses was hiding his face in terror. It had been many years since he fled for his life from Pharaoh and from his own sin of murder, and he was long settled now in Midian with a family and the steady job of sheep-tending. The traveller wondered how boring it must have been for Moses to swap his royal sceptre as a prince of Egypt, and all that it entailed, for a flock of sheep. But here he was, earning a quiet living, faithful to his God as part of the household of his father-in-law, Jethro the priest—and the whole applecart was about to be upset again, not by Moses this time but by God.

'You see, God had a job for Moses to do for him in Moses' old age,' continued DC. After all, hadn't he promised the children of Israel a land of their own all through the ages? You don't think he would renege on his principles just because an arrogant old bully like Pharaoh got in the way?' He smiled at her grin and continued his story. 'Down there, a man, no longer young, is about to be surprised by God in a manner he could not have imagined, and called to go where he least wanted to go, to perform a task for the Boss that most sane people would consider impossible. Moses thought so himself until God stepped into the equation, and the rest, as they say, is history.'

DC took her hand and directed her gaze away from Moses. 'In your century, Trav, slavery has long since been abolished, at least in the West, and a great deal of the challenges with which humankind once needed to wrestle just to survive no longer exist. But are you ready and willing to raise the call to "let my people go"? For God still requires his servants to walk from slavery into freedom. To escape the slavery of media image, and to throw off mass communication's dominion over time and opinion-moulding. To break free from the constant drive to *have more*, despite the fact that no matter how much they have, satisfaction still eludes them. To be released from the devastating effects of the endless search for pleasure or happiness or whatever else they might grasp to fill the aching void within them, which is the absence of true intimacy.'

She realized then that the call to Moses was the call to every Christian: it was a call to serve. Only oneness with God could even begin to approach the intimacy that Adam and Eve lost in the garden of Eden when, by their disobedience, they distanced themselves from the creator and from each other. In desperation for freedom, marriages are broken, children rebel against parents, and pews in churches stand empty. Fleeing from a sensation of loneliness, unfulfilment and deep inner pain, men and women, old and young, run so fast in the wrong direction that the very concept of 'sin' becomes blurred by the speed of their own flight. Like passengers looking out of the window on a runaway train, they are no longer able to focus on the passing scenery or direction of the journey: they lose the ability to understand that the answer to their quest will only be found when the direction is changed around—when they turn and seek after God.

Moses was given a new dream, which was a continuation of the dream his people had held in their hearts from God's promise to Abraham all those years before—a dream of identity, to be God's chosen people; a dream of a place to belong, a land flowing with milk and honey; a dream of deliverance from cruelty and bondage, a nation set free at last.

Was it so very different in her century? she wondered. Despite the improvements to Western life, were folk not still crying from the depths of despair for answers to the questions, 'Who am I? Where do I truly belong? And why me, Lord?'

Dear Father, show us the way to freedom. Open our eyes that we may see what holds us in bondage. Whatever other roles we play in life, reveal to us that our true identity can only be realized in relation to you. May we learn to seek full identity as 'children of God' more and more with each passing day. 'Let my people go!' you cry out, again and again, wherever and whenever we try to root our sense of belonging anywhere else but in you.

Father, thank you that the act of Christ on the cross releases the potential for immense healing and freedom from all kinds of bondage for each person who accepts your gift of salvation. I bring you today all that still binds me with chains of sin to a life not seeking you in intimacy and truth.

Let me be yours, Lord, let me belong. Please, in the name of Jesus, set me free—free to follow, free to live, free to serve as Moses served, wherever you send me. Amen

Saturday

DC'S DREAM

Then the angel showed me the river of the water of life, bright as crystal, flowing from the throne of God and of the Lamb through the middle of the street of the city. On either side of the river is the tree of life with its twelve kinds of fruit, producing its fruit each month; and the leaves of the tree are for the healing of the nations. Nothing accursed will be found there any more. But the throne of God and of the Lamb will be in it, and his servants will worship him; they will see his face, and his name will be on their foreheads. And there will be no more night; they need no light of lamp or sun, for the Lord God will be their light, and they will reign for ever and ever.

REVELATION 22:1–5

'One more dream, please, DC,' she pleaded after opening her eyes from prayer to find him staring out across a clear blue sky as though it was filled with a million items for his attention. He turned to examine her upturned face as though trying to read her thoughts again. 'What dream, Trav? What do you long for, that I might bring it to your slumber?'

'No, not mine, DC,' she replied, 'I want to hear your dream.' He looked puzzled. 'Don't you ever allow yourself dream-time? Surely there must be one that follows in your wake across endless skies and countless nights of flight?'

'Ah,' he nodded with understanding, 'I see what you're asking, Trav. But don't you know that I am from that place where every dream's fulfilment bathes for ever in the perfect light of God's enduring love? When dark night has ended, there is no longer need to dream of day, and in his presence there is no darkness—he is the light. Many ages will come and go before Christ returns a second time to earth and then, at the end of all ages, I will enjoy the dream come true with all God's children and celestial beings.'

His eyes looked into the middle distance then, as though he was seeing visions of tomorrow, sights she could not see.

'I wish you could look upon that river, Trav,' he whispered. 'Those shining, crystal-clear waters where you will glimpse the reflection of all that you have endured upon the earth and give yourself to the cleansing waters of life that flow from the very throne of God itself, where Jesus reigns at his right hand for ever. It will make sense then. All the questions, all the puzzles will make perfect sense to you. He has planted trees there, dear traveller, and one in particular, the tree of life, grows special leaves to heal the nations. You ask me what I'm impatient to observe? If I could, Trav, I would take a leaf from there and fly speedily to the earth and wipe each eye until grief could have no more power to stunt the lives of human dwellers upon your planet. With another leaf I would brush the heavy lids of all whose hatred and sectarian greed blinds them to the pain inflicted by their hands upon the innocents of ages still unborn. Then another, plucked by my impatient hand, would serve as ointment laid along the body of my Lord, the body of his Church, to address their mistakes and to mend the wounds and scars both borne and caused by Christ's beloved Bride in all her courts and institutions, until she rose anew, presented spotless to the Lamb.'

His eyes were shining now, not with tears but with joy, and he raised her to her feet. 'And you, dear friend, I'd take from you every step of agony you'll tread to a thousand Calvarys before your life is done. But...', and he let her hands fall once more, stepping back one stride as though to let another take his place, '...not yet, Trav, for this is just a borrowed dream, a pale reflection of what the Boss has planned for you at planet's end.'

The words of Paul came to her mind: 'What no eye has seen, nor ear has heard, nor the heart of man conceived... God has prepared for those who love him' (1 Corinthians 2:9).

'Your journey upon the earth is not in vain,' DC told her. 'No journey is. But you must walk it to its end. There are no short cuts, Trav—surely Christ's struggles in the wilderness have taught you that?'

She nodded, not without a little sadness, for the dream that he had visualized for her filled her heart and mind and soul with such sensations of beauty and peace that she wished above all else that she could bring it down to earth and play it loud and high and wide upon every jingling, jangling screen, filled as they were with earth's poor imitations of delight. Then all would see how tawdry they appeared beside the glory and the shining of the Lord.

But now she stood alone on foreign soil. Wherever she was at this moment, she could not tell. Even DC had gone, leaving her to walk and walk and walk where there seemed to be no mountains any more, or sea, or sky—just a long dirt path winding, curving, twisting on ahead as far as she could see. Suddenly she stopped and asked herself the question, 'Where is he now, the Lord?' and in a blinding panic wondered how she would ever catch up with him, where she'd left him in Nazareth. Even as she stood there wondering, lost and fearful, remembering the roads travelled by the dreamers—Hannah, Daniel, Jacob, Moses, Adam and his wife—a certainty swept through her being, tip to toe, that he would not leave her. Jesus had a dream to do the Father's will; he was with her now, unseen yet very near; and it would be his strength alone that kept her on the path to Calvary. She could not hear his voice but she knew that he smiled at her and prompted gently, 'Walk on.'

Dear God, I'm walking still and I know you'll never leave me. Give me your dreams to dream, that no invention, snag or distraction from the Bad 'Un will divert my path or deflect my intention to journey on with you.

I pray for Hannah's courage in her sacrifice, for Daniel's unbroken faithfulness, for Jacob's new beginning, and the challenge Moses heard from the startling interior of a burning bush. Give me eyes to see your guidance in every situation, ears to hear your voice when not a sound is uttered, and, like Eden's outcasts in all their disappointment, may I begin to plant for you a garden of my life. Amen

CALLED AND EQUIPPED

Sunday

FOLLOW ME

From that time Jesus began to proclaim, 'Repent, for the kingdom of heaven has come near.'

As he walked by the Sea of Galilee, he saw two brothers, Simon, who is called Peter, and Andrew his brother, casting a net into the sea—for they were fishermen. And he said to them, 'Follow me, and I will make you fish for people.' Immediately they left their nets and followed him. As he went on from there, he saw two other brothers, James son of Zebedee and his brother John, in the boat with their father Zebedee, mending their nets, and he called them. Immediately they left the boat and their father, and followed him.

MATTHEW 4:17–22

It was on a beautiful beach that she caught up with the Master again. Waves were gently lapping a pebbled shoreline. The shells were tiny and intricately marked. She had never seen so many delicate shapes before. On her local beaches shells were larger and didn't seem to be so varied in design. What a Maker, she thought, stooping down to collect a few and examine them closely as she washed the pearly, pink-edged, trumpet-shaped beauties in the water. This must be the Sea of Galilee, she thought, as she silently praised the creator for so much beauty.

Off to her right, two fishermen were casting nets into the sea, and she watched, fascinated, as their long sinewy arms flung the heavy material again and again out on to the top of the water. One of the men was thick-set and powerfully built, his head and shoulders turning almost a full circle as he projected the net a good distance beyond his reach. The other, a younger man, responded quietly to the orders barked by the older. 'What a team,' she mused, as the net was returned again and again, with fish wriggling and squirming for freedom. They certainly know what they're doing, she thought. They worked on tirelessly without a pause, until the Master halted them with a word.

Jesus had been watching too, patiently waiting until the nets were safely gathered. 'Peter,' he called. 'Andrew.'

She moved a little closer to overhear their conversation and was just in time to catch the end of it when he said, 'Follow me, and I will make you fishers of men.'

Suddenly she had a mental image of the big man, Peter, thinking he could fling a net over crowds of people and drag them into the kingdom like he did with fish, and the funny side of it made her smile. Poor man, she thought, fishing is what he knows best, but he's going to have to learn a great deal more about people before he can coax them into the kingdom. Yes, and a great deal more about himself too, she reckoned.

The three figures were moving off together now, leaving their nets abandoned to dry in the sun. Without a backward glance they walked side by side with Jesus, showing little concern for the fate of their equipment left behind. She imagined what might happen if businessmen in her era became so transfixed by the love and challenge of Jesus that computers no longer enslaved them for hours on end, that wealth and the dealings of commerce were given a subservient place when it came to time commitment and concentration. She had another mental image of locked tills and shelved agendas and abandoned sports cars blocking the motorways of the UK as folk heard a new and urgent call of Jesus to 'follow him' through the tangled and distorted paths of 21st-century living. They'd probably get arrested for causing an obstruction to the highway or consigned to a psychiatric hospital until they 'recovered'. She laughed at the thought of it. Mind you, watching those two newly recruited disciples striding along that beach in animated conversation with their Lord made her contemplate the consequences for Peter and Andrew if they had not chosen to follow, that day on the beach.

Dear Lord, show me what I still need to learn to be the follower you called me to be. Are there more skills I need to acquire? Is there additional cherished equipment I need to abandon?

Could an agenda of business or family or ambition be a shackle around my ankle to prevent my spiritual growth towards fulfilling your will?

Jesus, thank you that the fishing skills of Peter and Andrew were not wasted and that was not the last day on which those fishermen put out to sea. Please use the skills I have and show me how to place them in the right order of priority as I abandon my old life and walk on with you. Amen

Monday

TWIN OCCUPATIONS

Jesus went throughout Galilee, teaching in their synagogues and pro-claiming the good news of the kingdom and curing every disease and every sickness among the people. So his fame spread throughout all Syria, and they brought him all the sick, those who were afflicted with various diseases and pains, demoniacs, epileptics, and paralytics, and he cured them. And great crowds followed him from Galilee, the Decapolis, Jerusalem, Judea, and from beyond the Jordan.

MATTHEW 4:23–25

In the morning, while it was still very dark, he got up and went out to a deserted place, and there he prayed.

MARK 1:35

As Jesus continued his journey throughout Galilee, Trav became more and more excited, watching him heal many sick people. No disease was beyond his reach—epilepsy, chronic pain, paralysis, blindness, deafness, to name but a few. Even those demented in mind and spirit were no longer slaves to illness or evil when he set them free. The very worst that the Bad 'Un could manufacture was overcome by a word from the Lord.

In amazement and awe she stood quietly in the crowd, watching him take young children on his knee with such love and compassion and infinite patience that his disciples, whose numbers had now grown to twelve, protested at his allocation of valuable time.

'Where does he get the time from?' she mused out loud. 'He packs so much into the day.'

'Control,' came the answer from a voice behind her right shoulder.

'Oh, you again,' she muttered, somewhat peeved at DC's increasing habit of materializing whether she wanted him to or not. 'How can you accuse the Master of controlling things, when the whole point of his turning down the Bad 'Un's temptations is that he relinquished divine control while he was a human being upon the earth?'

'No, no, Trav,' smiled DC, 'not control of others, but discipline of himself.'

'How do you mean?'

'Remember how many demands were made on Jesus as he conducted his three-year ministry? As a carpenter, a preacher, a teacher, a healer, a brother, a leader, a son, a friend, a...'

'I get the picture, DC, what's your point?'

'Without discipline, his time would have been eaten up as if by a whirlwind, his mind would have been constantly under pressure, his body would have become exhausted and ill and he would have lived in a constant state of frustration at what still had to be done.' Then DC added as an afterthought, 'He might even have made lists.'

Trav shifted uneasily at the memory of the number of lists she kept pinned up everywhere at home, most of which got only superficially tackled before another even longer one joined them. She knew they could never all be dealt with in the way she longed to deal with them, not if she lived to be a hundred. They simply added to her continual state of frustration and hollow sensation of non-resolution.

'I am disciplined,' she sighed.

'Yes,' replied DC, 'none more than yourself. But do you control what other people think of you, or how much they commend you for the trouble you take, or how much they continue to think of you when you're gone?'

'I can't do any of those things, DC. No one could.'

'Exactly, Trav, yet how many people spend every minute of their time trying to control or enhance or trigger such responses from others? Jesus wasn't trying to please people, he spent every moment pleasing his Father in heaven. That's why he devoted so much of his daily time away from other human beings to concentrate on prayer—not only to feed and nurture his relationship with the Boss but also to examine what human traits were motivating him to do things. His prayer times helped him to get everything into perspective.'

The traveller watched as Jesus separated himself from a jostling group of miracle seekers and slowly set off up a nearby hill alone. She had seen him do this many times, often before dawn, and now she remembered—remembered the number of times she had heard her acquaintances protest, 'But I've no time for a specific quiet time, there's so much to *do!*' or, 'If you knew my kids you wouldn't expect me to have time to pray,' or, 'God wants us to get out there and change things, not waste time on developing our private spirituality!'

As she watched the Master day after day in private communion with his heavenly Father, the traveller realized that he was fuelling himself for action—taking on board the divine strength needed to discipline human attributes; opening his whole being fully to the life-force that comes only from God. Could she ever learn to do the same in the face of constant demands on her time?

'It's up to you, Trav,' DC whispered quietly as he slipped away. 'If you don't, this Lenten journey will be over and you still won't have time.'

Dear Father, how close will you let me come into your presence? Where have I been standing, up until now? Forgive my hesitation, my prevarication, my preoccupation with timetables, agendas and deadlines at the expense of your call to a deeper relationship with you.

Show me what I can 'edit' from my life. Show me which duties are heaven-sent and which are not. Meet with me on a level I had previously been too busy to discover. Amen

Tuesday

THE BIGGER PICTURE

Now a certain man was ill, Lazarus of Bethany, the village of Mary and her sister Martha. Mary was the one who anointed the Lord with perfume and wiped his feet with her hair; her brother Lazarus was ill. So the sisters sent a message to Jesus, 'Lord, he whom you love is ill.' But when Jesus heard it, he said, 'This illness does not lead to death; rather it is for God's glory, so that the Son of God may be glorified through it.' Accordingly, though Jesus loved Martha and her sister and Lazarus, after having heard that Lazarus was ill, he stayed two days longer in the place where he was.

JOHN 11:1–6

On they journeyed, the Lord followed closely by the traveller. From Galilee to Tyre and Sidon, and back again. To Judea beyond Jordan, and back again through Samaria. On and on and on, the traveller hearing parables and witnessing wonderful miracles and fearing, all the while, what was up ahead for the one she followed. Three years passed in the Lord's earth-time, but to her it seemed like a mere wisp of mist floating across the sea. Time itself was distorted between the ancient and modern centuries and she found herself only too quickly stepping behind him towards Jerusalem.

Would he stop for a rest at Bethany as he often had done in the past? she wondered. The family of three there were close to Jesus in friendship and trust. They had hosted many a 'teach-in', and many a celebration for him. But what he seemed to cherish the most in that house was the homely feeling of acceptance and love from the two sisters, Martha and Mary, and their brother Lazarus. Perhaps Jesus received there something that he dared not accept from his own brothers and sisters, whose unbelief and jealousy had more than once expressed itself in conflict in the past (Matthew 12:46–50).

This thought had only just passed through the traveller's mind when the turn Jesus took in the road ahead convinced her that he was indeed headed for Bethany. She began to feel her step becoming lighter. Those desserts of Martha's would start any mouth watering and she always looked forward to a visit there, even though she couldn't get a bite of that delicious food. Just to see her Master tucking into it with relish gave her a sense of glee.

It was then that she heard something which she found hard to believe. It came after the disciples had been muttering together on the return journey to Judea, seeming to be extremely nervous about Jesus going in that direction. They feared the reaction of the Jewish authorities, who had already made several hostile overtures in Jesus' presence. Suddenly and with great sadness Jesus said, 'Our friend Lazarus has fallen asleep, but I go to awake him out of sleep.' The others didn't understand at first that Jesus meant he had died. The traveller knew—she remembered this passage well from scripture—but she was suddenly stopped in her tracks by the realization that the Bible had indicated that Jesus had received a message from the sisters at Bethany and then delayed his journey there by two days. Had she been asleep when that message arrived? Could he really have known and yet delayed his coming to help? Yes, indeed, she began to realize that he had, and it made no sense to her at all. Wouldn't a close friend of long standing take precedence over most other items on his agenda?

He had given his disciples a bit of a conundrum to solve when they had questioned his reasoning and also his wisdom in returning now to an area where he would be at risk of arrest from the Jewish authorities. More and more she realized that Jesus' agenda was motivated by his Father in heaven over and above the circumstances in which he found himself, or even the emotional pressures that his human psyche imposed upon him. There was some bigger picture of which the disciples were ignorant. Jesus was moving towards an event that would change the life expectancy of humankind for ever. His was an eternal perspective, but he did not forget his friend Lazarus. Indeed, Lazarus himself had a part to play in this bigger picture.

As she listened to the Lord's conversation with his puzzled disciples, it reminded her of something she had heard him say once before to his followers. 'We must work the works of him who sent me, while it is day; night comes, when no one can work' (John 9:4). Jesus had been sent by God to do his will, in his time, in his way—and already the Lenten journey had begun. Already Jesus was on his way towards Jerusalem. When Thomas spoke with such loyalty and conviction, she felt her whole body go cold with fear. 'Let us also go, that we may die with him,' brazened the disciple whom she recognized as 'doubting Thomas'. With hindsight she remembered the unbelief of Thomas after the crucifixion and how he and the other disciples had fled in fear from the garden of Gethsemane.

Dear Father, we are going to fail him, aren't we? Again and again we fail him. All my good intentions, genuine efforts and real devotion fall so short of the mark. I don't even meet the standards I set myself, let alone those set by the example of Jesus.

It's frustrating, it's demoralizing, it's humiliating. It makes me ashamed and angry all at the same time. It makes me feel like giving up.

But wait, you didn't give up on those original disciples. You entrusted the establishment of your Church to them. I'm sorry, Lord, for all those times I have fallen short. Let's start again, can we? In your strength I think I can keep going. The day is short; let's journey on. Amen

Wednesday

A SHARED GRIEF

When Mary came where Jesus was and saw him, she knelt at his feet and said to him, 'Lord, if you had been here, my brother would not have died.' When Jesus saw her weeping, and the Jews who came with her also weeping, he was greatly disturbed in spirit and deeply moved. He said, 'Where have you laid him?' They said to him, 'Lord, come and see.' Jesus began to weep. So the Jews said, 'See how he loved him!' But some of them said, 'Could not he who opened the eyes of the blind man have kept this man from dying?'

JOHN 11:32–37 (READ ALSO VV. 17–31)

Standing helplessly at the tomb of Lazarus, the traveller would almost have swapped places with Mary and her sister Martha, if she could. What she witnessed was an interchange between the sisters and Jesus of the greatest intimacy—the intimacy of shared grief.

All around, mourners went through the normal, traditional rites of sympathy and wailing. Quite a crowd had gathered because the family was well known and also, living as they did only a few miles from the capital city, their home was often a stopping-off place for those journeying to Jerusalem as Jesus and the disciples themselves often did.

Martha was the first sister to meet Jesus before he reached the house, affirming her faith in his power and in the friendship that existed between Lazarus and Jesus. Or was she blaming him for his late arrival? After all, they had sent for Jesus before Lazarus was dead. No, wait, the traveller moved closer and heard Martha continue: 'But even now I know that God will give you whatever you ask of him.' Martha knew that recovery was beyond hope, because four days in the tomb meant that the spirit which the Jews believed to hover over a dead body for an initial three days would certainly be gone by now. Besides, it was Martha herself who acknowledged the advanced stage of decomposition that the body had already reached. The traveller wondered whether her hope was in a miracle, or whether she was expressing confidence in the Master's ability to help herself and Mary, who had not been able to leave the house to meet him yet.

Trav's heart quickened when she heard Jesus whisper, 'Your brother will rise again.' Surely now Martha would dare to hope; surely now she could imagine the unimaginable. But the poor woman, distraught by recent events, could only interpret his words in the light of the cold facts around her. Of course she believed that Lazarus would rise at judgment day. Didn't the Pharisees teach that the righteous would rise? Her brother was a good man; she believed that resurrection day would come to all good folk. Trav was almost holding her breath now in anticipation of Jesus' reply. 'I am the resurrection and the life,' she heard him say. 'Those who believe in me, even though they die, will live, and everyone who lives and believes in me will never die.'

Once Martha had acknowledged her belief in the Lord as Christ, God's Son, Jesus asked her to bring Mary to him. More people followed Mary from the house to where Jesus was waiting for her, and heard her reiterate Martha's cry: 'Lord, if you had been here, my brother would not have died.' The Lord married his grief with hers and he wept.

It was almost too much for the traveller, standing there where Mary and Jesus had moved closer to the tomb, standing there watching her Master give way to tears of such grief that the onlookers said, 'See how much he loved him.' She wanted to fling her arms around him in comfort. She felt such anger that he had not come sooner; and she felt anger in him too. She knew no Greek, so she was unaware of the anger evident in the original language of the Gospel writer's words, 'He was greatly disturbed in spirit and deeply moved.' But she knew what she saw—a deeply grieving man with anger mixing through tears of grief. She had no way of knowing why he was angry or with whom. Was he angry with himself for not coming sooner? No, he was doing God's will. Was he angry with

Martha and Mary for their words, and did he think they were passing blame to him? But his response to them was one of comfort and love. Did he feel he was about to be forced into performing a miracle that would subsequently be used against him? She could not guess at the answer, but she knew this—everyone who has ever lost a loved one struggles with bereavement as Jesus struggled. Feelings of pain at the loss, and often emotions of anger, come to the surface at such times.

The traveller began to cry herself. 'Oh Jesus,' she whispered, 'you know, you care, you understand what we've been through.' At that moment she would gladly have swapped places with Mary and felt his comforting presence, his shared grief, his power to change things.

Dear Lord, weep with me in all the broken places of my life. Stand firm at my side when everything I've loved lies in tatters at my feet.

You who know both sorrow and anger and yet have not given way to the destruction of despair or the evil of vengeful feelings, please temper my anger with love and gentleness of spirit. Please touch the emptiness of loss and fill it full of your promises that tomorrow there is more to be said and much more to be lived for you. Amen

Thursday

A PROMISE KEPT

Then Jesus, again greatly disturbed, came to the tomb. It was a cave, and a stone was lying against it. Jesus said, 'Take away the stone.' Martha, the sister of the dead man, said to him, 'Lord, already there is a stench because he has been dead four days.' Jesus said to her, 'Did I not tell you that if you believed, you would see the glory of God?' So they took away the stone. And Jesus looked upward and said, 'Father, I thank you for having heard me. I knew that you always hear me, but I have said this for the sake of the crowd standing here, so that they may believe that you sent me.' When he had said this, he cried with a loud voice, 'Lazarus, come out!' The dead man came out, his hands and feet bound with strips of cloth, and his face wrapped in a cloth. Jesus said to them, 'Unbind him, and let him go.'

JOHN 11:38–44

Even though the traveller knew what was about to happen, nothing could rob her of the intense sensation of release of burden and the surge of joy that filled her body, mind and soul as Jesus brought Lazarus alive from that cave.

She was watching Mary's face as it happened. Martha had turned slightly away, covering her mouth with her shawl in anticipation of the expected putrid odour as Jesus asked for the stone that sealed the cave to be removed. Martha's mind was on smells—always practical to a fault— Jesus' mind was on resurrection, but the traveller was watching Mary. The

Bible did not describe how Mary reacted and nor could the traveller. It was a realization of such joy and faith, relief and shock, love and exhaustion, that no words could capture the moment.

Mary had heard what Trav had heard when Jesus said, 'Father, I thank you for having heard me.' He was thanking God for the answer to his prayer before he had even given the command to Lazarus to 'come out'. Wasn't this the moment for faith to kick in? Isn't it while hope still lies buried in the tomb that faith justifies its existence? To know Jesus had thanked and trusted the Father was to see hope come staggering, smelly and disoriented, from the grave, waiting to be released from bonds of decay and abandonment.

Jesus had glorified his father, Lazarus had obeyed the Lord's command (even though he still looked a mess), but there was one more task to be done, and Jesus delegated it to someone else. 'Unbind him, and let him go,' he commanded. Tending to the dead was traditionally women's work, and two particular women standing by needed desperately to feel the healing balm of work to do for Lazarus in order to recover fully from all the anger and pain and loss of the past number of days. Trav did not need to witness who was releasing Lazarus from his funeral bindings to know that Jesus, once again, knew exactly what was needed to aid traumatized people as they emerged from suffering.

She did not follow the jubilant group back to that house in Bethany which had been the focus for so many gatherings and celebrations and restful visits for Jesus throughout his ministry. Instead, Trav lingered awhile by the empty tomb. The smell still hovered in the hot, eastern air. Some of the scraps of cloth had fallen at her feet where Lazarus had shaken them off impatiently as he walked free. She thought of the journeys that some of her friends would be making at home, right now—journeys through bereavement, transferring blame to others, racked with guilt, bowed low with pain of loss, seething with anger, filled with confusion at the maelstrom of conflicting and fluctuating emotions attacking their peace of mind, challenging their rationality, shaking their faith. She thought of their broken hearts, their inability to pray or to think or to make sense of what was happening to them.

Suddenly a great wave of empowerment swept through her being as the realization dawned. It was the same Jesus. This sweet humanity and powerful divinity all rolled into one was standing right now at their side, in their time, more powerfully, more 'there' for them than he could even have been for Martha and Mary. Because for them he had already conquered death and walked from his own tomb, and was no longer restricted by time or space or the limitations of a human body. Jesus, who knew exactly what to do for broken hearts and bereaved souls over two thousand years ago, longed to apply his physician's touch to the brokenness of her friends also.

She almost left then, almost turned towards home and fled back along the track to bring such good news, such potential healing power, to her time. But something stopped her. Up ahead, making their way towards Jerusalem, a small group of Jews who had been with Mary were making their way from the area in haste, and their muttered comments against Jesus filled Trav with dread. She must warn him, she thought, she must.

Dear Lord, thank you for the living, thank you for the life. Call me out from tombs of fear or despair, unbind my limbs, crushed by emotions too large to fight, by burdens too heavy to carry, by loss too deep to let go.

Unbind me and set me free, but, Lord, show me how to unloose the knots one at a time, that I may be your partner in the healing. Amen

Friday

LESSONS FROM THE PAST

Jesus therefore no longer walked about openly among the Jews, but went from there to a town called Ephraim in the region near the wilderness; and he remained there with the disciples.

Now the Passover of the Jews was near, and many went up from the country to Jerusalem before the Passover to purify themselves. They were looking for Jesus and were asking one another as they stood in the temple, 'What do you think? Surely he will not come to the festival, will he?' Now the chief priests and the Pharisees had given orders that anyone who knew where Jesus was should let them know, so that they might arrest him.

JOHN 11:54–57

She had stayed too long at the tomb. He had already left and the disciples with him. Retracing her steps towards the wilderness once more, she found him in Ephraim, not far from similar desert terrain which she had hoped to have escaped. At first she wondered if he had taken warning from someone else, because it was a much safer location for him and somewhere to be out of reach of the treacherous schemes of the Jewish authorities.

She liked the countryside and although it could hardly be compared with the lush green she was used to in the leafy suburbs at home, nevertheless there was a peace and security about Ephraim that helped her to relax a little.

Hardly a day passed without her noticing small groups of travellers moving through the surrounding countryside on their way to the capital. Soon the Passover would be celebrated, and many were making the journey early in order to perform the traditional rites of purification before the feast. It was a religious duty, and a great social gathering. The atmosphere of 'holiday' was everywhere. There was a feeling of anticipation in the air. Passover being the first feast of the Jewish religious year, it reminded Trav of the excitement that precedes Christmas. Except, there hasn't been a Christmas yet, she mused.

'Oh yes, there has,' said DC from just behind her.

'Are you reading my thoughts?' Trav challenged, with more than slight consternation in her voice, although by now she was getting used to him popping up from nowhere.

The dream carrier smiled patiently. 'I just thought it was worth reminding you that Jesus is already born and so there has been a Christmas, only no one recognizes it yet. It's only after Calvary that the full significance of why he's here dawns upon these poor followers of his,' he said, spreading his arms wide over the assembled group who sat listening to Jesus. 'I mean,' he continued, 'up to now the Master might as well have registered his CV as a wise teacher, miracle worker, and all-round general decent soul. He could join the club with all the many prophets who had gone before him.' DC turned away, muttering under his breath, 'They didn't listen to them either, half the time!'

'But DC,' Trav interrupted, 'these are willing students, faithful Jews, religiously hoping to celebrate the Passover. They want to do everything to keep themselves right with God. How could they miss the truth when it's right there under their very noses, living, breathing, teaching, eating with them?'

A shadow of sadness flicked momentarily across his face before he answered her gently, 'And what about the people of your century, Trav? They've got it all written down for them—his deeds, his sacrifice, his victory, his Holy Spirit freely available if accepted, not to mention over two thousand years of the ministry of his Church in all its varied parts. Do they accept this truth when it's right there under their noses?'

It must have been her downcast look that made him brighten his tone. 'Hey, Trav, lighten up, this is supposed to be a celebration,' he chirped, skipping in mid-air across an imaginary dance floor. 'It's the festival of freedom. That's why they're all going up that hill—the oldest of all the Jewish festivals. Moses himself commended it, and no good Jew would argue with Moses, would they?' he quizzed with a comical expression on his face.

She had to laugh then—he looked like a cross between a cheeky elf and the sage of all ages.

'Oh DC,' she laughed helplessly, 'sit down here beside me and tell me about it.'

'Well,' he said settling himself, 'three times a year, the men (those who are well enough, anyway) are expected to make a pilgrimage to the temple in Jerusalem. Passover is one of those times and for each family a sacrifice is made for their sins: a lamb is killed by each family and eaten later.' Trav shivered at the thought of so much bloodshed. 'You're right,' he agreed, 'it's a messy business. Yet it is always accompanied with great cleanliness. Before the Passover meal can be enjoyed, everything is cleaned—the house scrubbed from top to bottom, everything shining like a new kettle, and not one speck of leavened bread left behind. No one is allowed to eat leavened bread all week. Even roads are mended and bridges repaired, and every tomb that might contain a dead body is whitewashed so that no one will soil their eyes by looking on death on the way to the temple. That would make them unclean, from a religious point of view, at this time. Get the picture, Trav?'

She got the picture all right and it was making her feel very uncomfortable. She remembered Jesus' words to the scribes and Pharisees (Matthew 23:29)—the keepers of the law; the decent, educated, refined members of the Jewish synagogue and society; those above question in all observance and practice; the holy people, the ones who genuinely desired to do right by their God.

She pictured the pews at home, and it scared her. She remembered her own attempts at being godly according to all she had been taught throughout each church year, and it scared her. She recalled the million tiny rules she had taken care never to break, and the big ones too, and she shook in her hiking boots. Was she too, unknowingly, about to climb that hill to Jerusalem relying upon some sacrificial lamb of her own killing? Some dutiful 'spring-clean' that left inner cupboards of her life and spirit unopened and unexamined, while the forbidden pieces of leavened bread lay unpurged in the deep recesses of her heart and mind? What was the equivalent of unleavened bread in her own time and culture, she wondered, and, without any thought of blood at all, she shivered again.

Dear God, why does the Lenten journey have to be so messy? Couldn't we just turn up faithfully to church every Sunday, and do our religious duty like decent folk? Couldn't we listen and learn and sing all the right worship songs and go home and get on with the rest of our lives? After all, we know enough to teach Sunday school; we care enough to give to charity. What more can we do?

But Lord, the Jews of Jesus' time did all this. The Pharisees did it fervently, yet Jesus still had to come and journey to Calvary, because there is no more we can do. Only he can hunt out the hidden particles of sin in our lives. Only his sacrifice can cleanse fully.

Lord, inspect the inner recesses of my heart and soul. I want to draw back, I want to shield the dark corners from the light. What I don't know about won't hurt me, I think. But Jesus, it's hurting you, those tiny pieces of leavened bread wedged between skirting-board and floor and covered in cobwebs.

Give me strength, Lord, to allow them to come into the light of day, for I want to 'Passover', to pass over from death to life. If I don't let you change me, I will have spent too long at the tomb. Amen

Saturday

SETTING THE TABLE

Your boasting is not a good thing. Do you not know that a little yeast leavens the whole batch of dough? Clean out the old yeast so that you may be a new batch, as you really are unleavened. For our paschal lamb, Christ, has been sacrificed. Therefore, let us celebrate the festival, not with the old yeast, the yeast of malice and evil, but with the unleavened bread of sincerity and truth.

1 CORINTHIANS 5:6–8 (ALSO READ EXODUS 12:1–15)

'Are you praying, Trav?' DC's voice interrupted her thoughts.

'You know I am, DC,' she whispered through her tears.

'Don't you want to know more about the festival of freedom?'

She nodded, but her heart was heavy. What good was an ancient festival to her? she thought. Her Master was on his way to Calvary and there was nothing she could do to help him. The knowledge of it was almost too painful for her to bear. But DC was on his feet now, whirling round and about her, miming actions with great theatrical gusto. She watched him shake out an imaginary tablecloth and, with a great flourish, pretend to lay it before her on an imaginary table.

'Here is the family,' he declared, placing rocks in an arrangement around his imaginary table. 'This feast is very much a family meal. Can you see them, Trav? Are they all there?'

She named every rock inside her own head and smiled to think that not one member of the family was absent. It was a healing fantasy because even those who had already been taken from her to heaven she placed carefully in her mind's eye around the table.

'Good, good,' applauded DC as though he could see them too. 'Right then,' he said, gently placing his hands upon her shoulders and steering her to the top of the table. 'The men have just come home from the synagogue—here, here, and here—and now, Trav, you be mother.'

With a flourish he mimed the placing of candles upon the table and set an imaginary taper in her hand. 'Go, go,' he chattered excitedly, 'light the candles as every mum would light them on every eve of every sabbath.' He then mimed the pouring of wine and lifted that imaginary cup heavenward to bless it. As he poured four cups in all, he said, 'Each cup represents a promise of God from Exodus 6:6–7.' As if he was hearing the promises first-hand, he slowly spoke them aloud: 'I will free you; I will deliver you; I will redeem you; and I will take you as my people.'

Tears were still in Trav's eyes as the scene took vivid shape and form before her. She heard the youngest child ask the traditional question: 'Why is this night different from all other nights?' She heard the father figure tell the story of how God had delivered his children from the hands of the Egyptians. She watched as DC filled a fifth cup for Elijah who, by tradition, was expected to appear on Passover night to herald the coming of the Messiah.

She stared at the table that DC had painstakingly set for her in her imagination, visualizing the food. There was the hard-boiled egg, a sign of new birth for a new nation and later a sign of mourning when the temple was destroyed. Parsley was a sign of spring but also a representation of the hyssop used to sprinkle the lamb's blood on the doorposts, to warn the angel of death to pass over that home and leave the firstborn sons of the Hebrews in safety. Salt water represented the tears of the Hebrew slaves in bondage but also the salt of the Red Sea, their path to freedom. Bitter herbs for the bitterness of their captivity in Egypt—what vengeful thoughts these must represent. Lettuce—what little food was available for slaves was represented by a mere lettuce leaf. She thought of DC's mime of great promise, and the future hope of Elijah's cup, and of course, in modern times, the shank bone for the sacrificial lamb. The unleavened bread was there too, from the loving hands of someone without enough time to bake normal bread. Staring closer at the loaf, she realized that she was picturing a modern Passover, with the bread wrapped in supermarket packaging.

Instead of Egyptian mud, with which the slaves once toiled to make bricks for their masters, she was seeing a labourer in a building-site helmet, leaving a cement brick upon the table. She laughed at the image and turned, a little red-faced, to DC.

'I'm sorry, I couldn't help imagining...'

He interrupted her with his own cheerful laughter. 'That's great, Trav, that's the way to do it. You want to continue your Lenten journey in Christ's footsteps? Bring your tears to the table and find healing. Bring your starvation, as a slave to negatives and sin, and find his sustenance. Search for any bitterness, any nasty taste in your spiritual life, and weed it out, to be able to celebrate and enjoy the new wine of promise that Christ is bringing and, for the people of your time, has already brought about.

Dear Father, have I been ignoring your promises? In the midst of my suffering, have I seen only tears and forgotten the salty waters parting at the Red Sea? Have I embraced the bitter herbs and not spat out the bile? Have I mourned at many modern temples in my life and never fully recognized the signs of new life in Jesus?

Heavenly Father, can I light those Passover candles and welcome in your hope, not just for myself but for all who call me 'family' and even those who don't? I want to 'pass over', Lord. Take me gently but firmly through deep waters, that the sacrifice of my Master will not have been in vain for me. Amen

Week Four

THE COST

Sunday

A HIGH COST

Six days before the Passover Jesus came to Bethany, the home of Lazarus, whom he had raised from the dead. There they gave a dinner for him. Martha served, and Lazarus was one of those at the table with him. Mary took a pound of costly perfume made of pure nard, anointed Jesus' feet, and wiped them with her hair. The house was filled with the fragrance of the perfume. But Judas Iscariot, one of his disciples (the one who was about to betray him), said, 'Why was this perfume not sold for three hundred denarii and the money given to the poor?' (He said this not because he cared about the poor, but because he was a thief; he kept the common purse and used to steal what was put into it.) Jesus said, 'Leave her alone. She bought it so that she might keep it for the day of my burial. You always have the poor with you, but you do not always have me.'

JOHN 12:1–8

She found Jesus at Bethany again with his beloved friends Martha and Mary and Lazarus. There was some kind of party going on and the disciples were tucking into the supper. A strange, sweet smell hung in the air. It reminded her of the perfume counters in every huge department store she had ever been in, and Judas was wearing a face like thunder.

'Is that Mary I can see, sitting at Jesus' feet like a student rabbi? I thought only men were allowed to learn from a master in such a way,' she said to DC. But he had gone again, no doubt carrying a dream somewhere.

Moving further in to get a better look, she could see that Mary was wiping Jesus' feet with her hair. Now everything smelt of the ointment that she had obviously poured over those feet. It was dripping from his toes, it was spreading across the floor, her hair was covered in it and beginning to look matted. Trav was wondering how she would ever get the smell out when Judas exploded in a fit of rage. Was he jealous of Mary's close relationship with Jesus, or trying to shift the blame in view of his own role in dealing with the accounts?

Jesus did not seem in any hurry to reject Mary's wonderful expression of extravagant love. He was more concerned about the insincere sentiments of Judas. Trav wondered how many of those present recognized the hint about his own forthcoming death: no one seemed eager to comment on it. But as everyone present stared in puzzled disbelief at the intimate scene in front of them, her eyes were on Mary—the brunt of jealousy and scornful remarks, persecuted by false accusations, her motives misunderstood and challenged by those who ought to have known better, now crouched at the Lord's feet, financially poorer by who knows how much. The expensive love token was spilt upon the ground, her hair matted with its remains and her future threatened by the treasurer of the group wielding all his power of control. What a costly act indeed for Mary to serve Jesus in this way!

Trav couldn't help remembering the story from the Old Testament when King David had refused to offer a sacrifice to God that had cost him nothing (2 Samuel 24:24).

On the way to Calvary she realized that every step was costly for Jesus, every insult, jibe and act of violence a blood-wound to the heart—and here he was on one of the days when he could relax, when he was relatively safe from the authorities, at rest with his friends, and Satan had managed to use his own followers as a channel of attack. Perhaps, for the Bad 'Un, Mary's act of costly sacrifice reminded him of the ultimate sacrifice that Jesus was prepared to make to do his Father's will. Judas' anger originated from a darker power than himself but it was Judas who allowed himself to be used in this manner. Trav was beginning to have her vision expanded in terms of the cost of following in Jesus' footsteps. If Jesus had not withheld any costly thing to save her—no, not even his life—could she afford to hold back anything that she treasured in cost or time or relationship, to serve him fully, as Mary had served, with extravagant love?

Dear Lord, not this, please don't ask me to give up this, on the way to Calvary. I love it so dearly, I need it so deeply, I depend upon it so much. From this alone comes fulfilment and enjoyment and a sense of who I am. From this comes my identity, my peace of mind, my orientation of where I am in life. In this I feel content.

Like Mary, staring in the mirror and imagining the uses that that sweet-smelling substance could serve—the men it might attract by the wearing of it, the finance it might generate by the selling of it, the security it might protect by the saving of it, and the people it might help by its donation to charity. What dreams and hopes and plans were shattered by the spilling of it, deliberately, over tired and dusty feet? What loved one's funeral was lessened because it was not there to anoint them when the time came?

Jesus, you first, I give all to you. Loosen my grip on anything that hijacks my sacrificial love for you. May nothing distract me from that goal of full devotion to you.

Please, Lord, may I not offer you that which costs me nothing. Amen

✢

Section Two Introduction

TO SLEEP, PERCHANCE
TO DREAM

At first she did not realize she was sleeping. Yes, she could remember getting to bed. It had been a tiring day and she had thought long and hard about the incident with the ointment before falling asleep, but standing here, in her own bedroom at home, surrounded by all her familiar things, she did not at first realize she was sleeping. For a moment she struggled to remember how she had got back home and reached over to the side of the bed to check her alarm clock. Nothing happened. Her hand did not move and her eyes saw no clock.

'I'm asleep,' she said to herself, expecting no answer.

'You certainly are,' came the surprise reply from a familiar voice.

'DC, is that you? Are you turning up in my dreams now?'

'Where else would you expect a dream carrier to be, Trav?' came the reply, but she still couldn't see him anywhere. 'It's your lucky night, girl, I've got a dream for *you!*'

Suddenly the bedroom was full of objects, on the bed, strewn across the floor, draped over the dressing table—and right there on top of the bookcase, balanced precariously between two weighty volumes, was a casket of pure nard. She began to move towards it when DC's voice halted her.

'Never mind the ointment,' he said. 'You already know what to do with that. It's all the other things from which you must choose.'

'Choose? You mean, I get to keep one?'

'If you like,' he chirped, still invisible. 'You will come across them soon on your way to Calvary. If you like, you can select one to help the Master on his journey.'

Her pulse quickened. 'You mean I can actually make a difference to his journey? I'm allowed to affect the time-line in some way by using one item from this lot?'

'If you like,' repeated DC. 'But only one, and you must stay in character. That is, you must act as someone from his own era, not telling him where you are from, or what you are trying to do.'

Her eyes shone with excitement. She was actually going to be visible in his time, to be effectual on his route to Calvary. This is what she had wanted all along. At last her journey would not be in vain.

'Have a go, then,' said DC.

'But I want to wake up first. I need to get back to where he is now.'

'Sorry, Trav, not until you've had a practice. That's what this dream is all about—a rehearsal, if you like, for the real thing. Besides, you have to take quite a lot of time deciding which item to choose. I'll leave you to get on with it. Bye!'

Across her duvet lay a piece of bracken. It looked dirty and she brushed it to the floor in disgust. But that was nothing to the repulsion she felt at the sight of the hind legs of a fair-sized donkey protruding from her wardrobe as he contentedly champed away on her bright red feather boa. Running to rescue her party outfit, she stubbed her toe on a wooden goblet, out of which tumbled thirty pieces of silver. As she dived beneath the bed to recover the runaway coins, her hand took a nasty slash from the sharpest sword she had ever encountered. Come to think of it, she had never encountered such a weapon in her century before. Bleeding, and more than a little disorientated, she rushed to the dressing-table, where a basin was perched with a handy towel draped just where she needed it. Funny, she hadn't left either of them there, and this basin was certainly something better than plastic.

Wrapping the towel around her cut hand, she collapsed in her bedroom chair exhausted, only to leap to her feet with a howl, for there, where her posterior had just been, rested what she could only describe as a branch of thorns roughly woven into a circle. This dream was rapidly turning into a nightmare.

'Get on with it, Trav,' she heard, the dream carrier's voice echoing from a great distance, fading to silence. Oh yes, she thought, it's all right for him, he doesn't have to make a choice.

Carefully she lined the objects up and spread them across the floor—all except the donkey, which she secured firmly to the door handle with a chain of belts, carefully placing the basin underneath his rear end for obvious reasons. She was fond of her carpet. Oh boy, she thought, *now* what do I do, Lord?

Monday

FIRST THINGS FIRST

After he had said this, he went on ahead, going up to Jerusalem.

When he had come near Bethphage and Bethany, at the place called the Mount of Olives, he sent two of the disciples, saying, 'Go into the village ahead of you, and as you enter it you will find tied there a colt that has never been ridden. Untie it and bring it here. If any one asks you, "Why are you untying it?" just say this, "The Lord needs it."' So those who were sent departed and found it as he had told them. As they were untying the colt, its owners asked them, 'Why are you untying the colt?' They said, 'The Lord needs it.' Then they brought it to Jesus; and after throwing their cloaks on the colt, they set Jesus on it.

LUKE 19:28–35

The donkey had to go. Believe me, as far as she was concerned, *the donkey had to go!* She determined that this would be the first thing she would try to use to change the situation for the Master—if only to get it out of her bedroom. Dream or no dream, it really had no business being there, she reckoned.

It was a real struggle for Trav to haul the donkey out of her house. It had never been ridden and had a mind of its own. In her dream the scenery changed and she and the donkey were making slow progress along an ancient street in glorious non-cooperation. Out of frustration she began muttering angrily to the animal as they went. 'Stubborn? That's not the word for you! Do you have to be such a typical ass? Why did he have to choose an unbroken colt, anyway? Surely a well-ridden camel would be easier to borrow, or a horse. Yes, it should have been a horse.'

Before she realized it, the Master was standing before her, a wry smile on his face, his hand outstretched to take the chain of belts she was using to pull the animal along. In her dream she couldn't even focus upon Jesus but only struggled with the donkey. 'Here you are,' she grumbled. 'This is a big mistake, Lord, really it is. A camel would be trained; a horse would at least have a saddle. Then, as if inspired, she broke into a eulogy about horses. How comfortable they were to ride, how obedient (in comparison to a donkey), how much more dignified, with so much more status afforded to them, faster too and more graceful—in fact (she reckoned) fit for a king.

The look on his face made her stop talking. It was one of wisdom and sadness, of gentleness and humour, and she even thought she saw a twinkle in his eye at her protestations.

In an instant a book lay open in the palms of her hands and the dream had taken him from view. She stared down at the Bible in her hands, opened at Zechariah 9:9, and read, 'Lo, your king comes to you; triumphant and victorious is he, humble and riding on an ass, on a colt the foal of an ass.'

So nothing else would have done, Lord, she thought to herself—not if it was to fulfil the prophecy. Besides, a horse is associated with war and you are a prince of peace. For a few seconds she felt ashamed at her own stupidity, but not for long, because just behind her right ear a donkey was braying loudly. 'Oh no, not you again!' she muttered under her breath, swinging round to see DC grinning broadly as he led the donkey towards her.

'No, Trav,' he replied, 'it's not the same one, but would *you* ride it? At home, at work, at leisure, could you take the way of humility, walking paths of peace when all around are in conflict? Choose now, Trav. Is it to be the pattern of TV soap operas you choose to follow, or the example of your Lord and saviour? It's a pride thing, Trav. Can you take control of yours?'

She wasn't sure whom she was happiest to be rid of at that point, DC or the stubborn ass, but finding herself back in her bedroom again she knelt in prayer to her Master.

Dear Lord, how many faces does pride wear? How many justifications does it manufacture for its existence? And the wounds hurt so badly when it is attacked. It weaves a cloak of assumed righteousness about itself when anger summons it to the fray, and hides in caverns of isolation when failure tarnishes its metal. The monster of fear will enlist its patronage rather than submit to love. It straddles the twin hills of prejudice and intolerance to make itself taller than those who might dare to challenge its position, and it makes such children of us when our adult toys are taken by another.

Pride is the fruit that Eve just had to eat, rather than trusting her loving creator that all would be well and believing that he would not have placed her in a garden that was second best to anything in all creation.

Please train me in the art, the grace and the growing steps of obedience that will one day make you proud of me. Amen

Tuesday

FLAGS OF ADORATION

'Tell the daughter of Zion, Look, your king is coming to you, humble, and mounted on a donkey, and on a colt, the foal of a donkey.'

The disciples went and did as Jesus had directed them; they brought the donkey and the colt, and put their cloaks on them, and he sat on them. A very large crowd spread their cloaks on the road, and others cut branches from the trees and spread them on the road. The crowds that went ahead of him and that followed were shouting, 'Hosanna to the Son of David! Blessed is the one who comes in the name of the Lord! Hosanna in the highest heaven!'

MATTHEW 21:5–9 (READ VV. 1–11 IN TOTAL)

She had seen plenty of flag-waving before. But now, standing amid a huge crowd of pushing, jostling people in her dream, she couldn't believe what they were waving. Moving along Jerusalem's narrow thoroughfares, anything and everything was being waved in the air, branches of every tree imaginable, even coats were being flourished and flung with abandon on the ground. And there she stood with her pitiable piece of bracken. She wished it could have been at least a fresh palm branch like the ones brandished by the children as they skipped along singing, 'Hosanna!'

Crowds were not new to Trav. They were highlighted constantly in her time, through the media's insatiable appetite for news. She'd seen the mass hysteria of a football match, the pain of refugees fleeing in their thousands in the wake of a natural disaster, and, in Northern Ireland, flags of every creed and colour being used to protest, or to wound, or to stake a claim to land that belonged only to God. How people disappear in a crowd: individuals become faceless, responsibility becomes disembodied, we can just blame 'the crowd'.

She studied the faces of the children, pushing and shoving all around her, their eyes full of excitement and innocent glee. They were welcoming their hero, the man who told great stories, who performed miracles, who did not push them away when adults were around—the man the adults said would set the country free from the oppression of the government's crippling taxes and domination. Maybe if they got close enough they'd see him do a magic trick, or he might even lift them up for a ride on his donkey. Who needed a footballer to cheer for, or a pop star to scream for, when Jesus was in town?

All the while, the Master rode on slowly along the narrow, stony avenues towards the temple, with a determined look on his face. Trav had to fight the surge of the surrounding bustle to push her way to the side of the donkey. 'Don't go, Lord,' she pleaded. 'Please don't go. These people don't understand what you are trying to do. Look,' and she extended her wind-burnt bracken so that he could see it, 'all the branches and flags, they're just so much burnt bracken, scorched by the heat of the people's own agendas.' She began to snap off brittle fragments of her bracken and let them flake away before his eyes as he rode on. 'They won't be faithful, Lord, these people will not stand by you. When the chips are down you can't rely on one of them. Don't go.'

They had reached the outer perimeter of the temple and Jesus was dismounting without haste. As he turned his eyes to look into her face, a thrill of such joy reverberated through her to her very soul. They were the eyes of someone who knew exactly what he was doing and knew too much to stop. The compassion she saw in those eyes was not for himself but for her. She knew that he was not about to speak; instead he raised his hand, pointing to the outer portal of the temple; and signalled for her to follow him in.

Without difficulty she gained admission. The outer courtyard was a kind of bustling marketplace, rather like the Sunday outdoor markets that she avoided at home. They always made her uncomfortable, knowing that there were better things to do for God on Sunday than buy and sell. She recognized the items on show as being legitimate purchases for any good

Jew coming to make sacrifice at the altar—pigeons, and many kinds of animals. There were money changers too, lots of them, and she wondered how many were taking advantage of poverty-stricken worshippers after their long pilgrimage. Once you entered the temple, these stallholders had certainly cornered the market in essential religious items and the exchange rate at the money tables seemed none too reasonable. As women were allowed in this part of the temple, Trav was able to move freely; and the more she examined, the less this place felt like a place of prayer. She might just as well have been in the high street at home, and it galled her greatly.

She wasn't the only one. The crash of the first table being overturned made her swing round in consternation. Jesus, strong carpenter's muscles flexing, legs striding with ease, a terrible pain of disappointment and horror in his taut expression, was putting an end to this desecration of the sabbath, this exploitation of the people, this defilement of his Father's house.

Dear Father, what have we done to your house? How sacred is it now? How much do we cherish one day in seven, protecting it from the secular ravages, stresses and duties of the previous week?

Have I walked through the courtyards of my sabbath and cleansed it totally and without reservation, as Jesus did? If he physically visited my time and place, what would he overturn? How can I help him, Father, and when should I start?

Every moment I delay, I see the pain and horror in his eyes. I can't reduce the suffering he endured two thousand years ago, but he has put me where I live to change things on my own doorstep.

Give me courage, Lord, for those around me will not like it. But then, they didn't like it much in your day either, did they, Lord? Amen

Wednesday

LISTEN TO THE CHILDREN

The blind and the lame came to him in the temple, and he cured them. But when the chief priests and the scribes saw the amazing things that he did, and heard the children crying out in the temple, 'Hosanna to the Son of David,' they became angry and said to him, 'Do you hear what these are saying?' Jesus said to them, 'Yes; have you never read, "Out of the mouths of infants and nursing babies you have prepared praise for yourself"?' He left them, went out of the city to Bethany, and spent the night there.

MATTHEW 21:14–17

She didn't hang about the temple courtyard for long. Just long enough to witness the eager stream of sick people pouring into the courts of that huge building, seeking healing from Jesus. She wondered why he didn't leave, and leave fast, after his exceedingly practical demonstration of how things ought to change. Of course he would heal those who needed help, of that she had no doubt; but what she wanted to know was what was going on in the minds of the chief priests and scribes who had just witnessed their sanctuary disrupted and were listening, even now, to the adoration of many children's voices singing the Lord's praises, and proclaiming him to be the Son of David. Wouldn't that mean that he was heir to King David's throne?

Surely, to an ordinary Jew of the day, a king would take precedence over a priest—and especially if he claimed to be the long-awaited Messiah. No wonder she found the temple priests and scribes huddled together in consultation. In her dream she dared not go too close for fear of being seen, so it was a garbled conversation that she overheard. Anxious tones floated on the air like cinders from the fires of envy. She caught a scrap here, a phrase there—nothing was clear. But she gleaned that they saw Jesus as a threat to their position. He was unqualified, theologically untrained, a carpenter, and from Galilee of all places. Not much good comes from there, they thought. He had no right to teach the people. That was their job; their role was in jeopardy. Now today he had set the cat among the pigeons—quite literally, one of them quipped, and she was glad that at least somebody had a sense of humour.

But he couldn't go insulting their 'customers' like this. Much-needed revenue for the temple came from those market stallholders and all the business they did. How were they going to meet their quota, or afford repairs to the building, or even draw a salary, if revenue dropped? Besides, he's playing at God, isn't he, doing miracles in broad daylight? 'Yes,' said the scribe with the sense of humour, 'but what *harm* has he done?'

A stunned silence followed for several seconds. Heads moved closer together, tongues clicked rapidly, suggestions she could not hear were thrown into the ring and rejected with shakes of the head. Then, finally, like one discovering the holy grail, a raised voice proclaimed, 'Lazarus!'

'Yes,' barked another, 'people think he raised him from the dead. We can't have that.'

'He claims to be able to forgive sins,' said another. 'Only God can do that.'

It was almost as if the huddled group breathed a corporate sigh of relief. They parted in good spirits.

With a heavy heart she returned to the street where small knots of people were still slowly labouring up the hill to the temple. Perched on a tethering-stone, one without a camel attached, Trav tuned in again to the sound of innocent children's laughter. Half a dozen or so were playing nearby as their parents prepared to eat a meagre snack.

Jesus had welcomed the praises of the children and had firmly aligned himself to the creative role of his Father God, quoting from Psalm 8 where the same praises were addressed to God himself. The traveller, weary from her journey thus far, rested within her temporary dream state and worshipped the Father in rest and sleep.

'O Lord, our Sovereign, how majestic is your name in all the earth!'

Dear God, thank you for being here for me. When attacks come and when enemies rage, thank you for being still in control.

'You have set your glory above the heavens. Out of the mouths of babes and infants you have founded a bulwark because of your foes, to silence the enemy and the avenger.'

Help me remember that I worship alongside angels and archangels, and yet the children have got it right, for their worship is unself-conscious, trusting and without fear, whatever the cost. Forgive my building of defences when the only protection I really need is trust in you.

'When I look at your heavens, the work of your fingers, the moon and the stars that you have established, what are human beings that you are mindful of them, mortals that you care for them? Yet you have made them a little lower than God, and crowned them with glory and honour.'

In fear I forget to look upwards. Frightened, I miss out on all the beauty and wonder you have created for me to enjoy. I don't deserve your care for me, your interest in my little life, your great sacrifice of love on my behalf. From where did you get the greatness to stoop so low to raise us high?

'You have given them dominion over the works of your hands; you have put all things under their feet, all sheep and oxen, and also the beasts of the field, the birds of the air, and the fish of the sea, whatever passes along the paths of the sea.'

Poor donkey, I wasn't much good for him, was I, Lord? So busy chasing my own deadlines to 'help' the Saviour that I missed the significance of the sacred trust of all things 'under my feet', things and creatures that you have entrusted to my care. Ah, Lord, and maybe people too. Grant me grace to serve all those you put within my way.

'O Lord, our Sovereign, how majestic is your name in all the earth!'

Help me to listen to the children, Lord. They got it right—Jesus and the Father are one. That wonderful word, 'Hosanna'—'save me'—to them on the entry to Jerusalem was no more or less than an exuberant shout of joy. Joyfully I shout too: thank you for your majestic love!

Thursday

THE MEAL

On the first day of Unleavened Bread, when the Passover lamb is sacrificed, his disciples said to him, 'Where do you want us to go and make the preparations for you to eat the Passover?' So he sent two of his disciples, saying to them, 'Go into the city, and a man carrying a jar of water will meet you; follow him, and wherever he enters, say to the owner of the house, "The Teacher asks, Where is my guest room where I may eat the Passover with my disciples?" He will show you a large room upstairs, furnished and ready. Make preparations for us there.' So the disciples set out and went to the city, and found everything as he had told them; and they prepared the Passover meal.

MARK 14:12–16

'Are you going to sleep for ever?' She heard DC's question as he gently shook her awake.

'Is it still a dream?' she asked, rubbing the sleep from her eyes.

'Not any more,' he sang out as he jumped aside and showed her the eastern scenery with a flourish, 'not unless you call all this time-travelling a dream also?'

'Don't confuse me, DC,' she laughed. 'This is hard enough for me as it is. I suppose I'm invisible again?'

'Yep,' he grinned.

'So what about the other five objects in my dream? Don't I get to try them out after all?'

He tapped his nose cryptically. 'We'll see, Trav, we'll see.'

'Stop being so mysterious, DC! Help me out here. Nothing I've attempted so far has been of any use whatsoever to the Master on this journey, and you didn't help with your dream.'

He looked somewhat crestfallen and she regretted taunting him, but he spoke before she could retract her sharp words.

'You didn't learn anything, Trav? Not about donkeys, or flags, or enemies, or children, or worship, or rest, or... Hey, where are you going? Don't you walk away from me, Trav!'

She was moving all right: something had caught her attention and she was hot in pursuit, with DC bringing up the rear.

'Hold on!' he called out, catching up, a trifle breathless. 'Where are you going?'

'Look,' she said, quickening her step, 'look, DC, a man carrying a water jar.'

'So? It's a thirsty land.'

'Yes, but didn't the women bring home the water in these days? Come on, DC, you ought to know that better than I do.'

'My, my.' DC sounded comical, shaking his head in mock astonishment. 'So the "new man" mentality didn't wait for the 20th century then, Trav, is that what you're saying?'

She flashed him a scathing glance and pointed to a small knot of disciples stepping forward to waylay the water carrier.

'See?' she exclaimed. 'It was a sign, I knew it had to be some kind of a sign. Jesus told them to look for a male water carrier, and here he is. I don't believe in coincidence when we're in God's will, DC, and this was no coincidence.'

The disciples and the man had entered a house with an upper room and she stopped at the door, hesitant to follow. 'This is it, isn't it, DC? This is *the* upper room. They are going to have the last supper here, aren't they? Jesus had already booked the room and now the disciples have come to prepare it, haven't they?'

'Well, why don't you go inside and see?' he retorted.

But she hung back with a mixed feeling of awe and dread restricting her progress. 'I can't go in, DC. Please don't make me go in,' she pleaded.

He knelt beside her where she had sunk back on to her knees on the dirt road. 'Why not, Trav?' he whispered softly. 'You're as much his guest as they are.'

Suddenly a welter of mixed emotions overwhelmed her. Dozens of times she had taken Communion in her home church—perhaps even hundreds by now; she had never counted. It was a regular routine, a blessed duty, sometimes even an inspiration, but here it was real. Here Jesus had reworked the Passover meal into a celebration of a freedom not from Egypt, but from death and slavery to sin. Here he would sketch them an outline of his own death and resurrection and command them to remember him always by enacting his sacrifice through engaging in this meal. What a drama, she thought; what a potent channel by which to commemorate him; what a powerful vow-bonding with the Saviour! How dare she intrude? She was not worthy; she was not ready. He would see how imperfect she was, invisible or not, she was sure of it.

DC gently took her hand and led her through the door and up the flight of steps to a moderately large room already furnished and prepared for the Passover. She saw again on the table all those elements mimed by DC when he had taught her about the original feast celebrated for centuries. But now she stared at the boiled egg and it was the destruction of Christ's body she mourned; the salt brought an experience of his tears to her eyes; the sight of the herbs evoked great bitterness in her breast over the treachery of those who plotted his downfall; and the lamb in the centre position on the table… she could not bear to look upon it. She was full of such pain and anger and guilt and fear that she did not even have the strength to flee from the room but stood, rooted to the spot, as the twelve disciples filed in, laughing and joking, to take their places casually at the table.

Dear Lord, how could they? How were they able to eat and drink and laugh and joke and listen and ignore and fail to understand what was happening that night in the upper room?

But Lord, forgive me, for don't we too fail to understand all the time, even though we ought to have the wisdom of hindsight? Next time I come to the table, help me to vow-bond with you. Amen

Friday

WITH ME

When it was evening, he came with the twelve. And when they had taken their places and were eating, Jesus said, 'Truly I tell you, one of you will betray me, one who is eating with me.' They began to be distressed and to say to him one after another, 'Surely, not I?' He said to them, 'It is one of the twelve, one who is dipping bread into the bowl with me. For the Son of Man goes as it is written of him, but woe to that one by whom the Son of Man is betrayed! It would have been better for that one not to have been born.'

MARK 14:17–21

It was a difficult task for the traveller to watch Judas enter that room with the other disciples and take his place at the table. If the dream she had previously experienced had taught her anything, it had reinforced for her the certainty that nothing she could do would change this time-line or assist Jesus in his journey. She longed to be able to cry out to him, to unmask the traitor in their midst, to alert the disciples to the danger. It was especially frustrating to watch Jesus reach over and offer Judas the opportunity to dip his bread into the tasty bowl with Jesus, a privilege normally reserved for a specially chosen friend by the chief guest at a banquet. Yet the gesture was taken by them as one of privilege, not of warning, despite a pretty large hint from the Lord himself.

Was the position of Judas so powerful, so established, so secure that none dared challenge his credibility? Or were the others so wrapped up in protesting their own irrefutability that they could not protect Jesus from the danger in their midst? she wondered. Then, as she gazed around those relaxed disciples, each protesting their undying loyalty in their own way, she remembered how each one had fallen short of even their own standards of discipleship before Calvary's destination was reached. Perhaps Jesus could not, would not, have exposed Judas for many reasons—not the least being the fact that he knew how all his team, except John, would desert him in his dying.

Who was truly 'with him' but his divine Father? Who deserved to sit at that table in sinless perfection but Jesus? Would anyone be worthy of such a meal, of such a promise, of such an eternity?

'Not yet,' she whispered aloud and mainly to herself. 'Not yet, Lord, until you have first undertaken to "passover".' She realized that only when his journey was over and his task completed in the Father's will could this table become no more a place of privilege or status, no more merely a religious duty or obedience to the law, no more a cosy gathering of like-minded members of a religious 'club', but what it was intended to be—a memorial, a cleansing of unworthiness, an enactment of future promise.

She slipped to her knees at the foot of the table where a space had been left for the house servant and, although she knew she could not be seen, she felt a part of this gathering. Unworthy, like them; confused, like them; ignorant of what her future held, as the disciples were ignorant of what lay up ahead for them. Wanting desperately to follow where the Master led, like them, and scared to imagine the worst. But like them she heard the voice of her Lord, felt his presence take control of the proceedings, shared the atmosphere of being at one with her surroundings in the common meal together. If only for a short while, she was at peace.

Dear Lord, forgive me for not resting in your presence, for always wanting to anticipate the future and make plans, to take precautions, to secure it ahead of time.

Teach me how to live in the 'now', in that place where my chief responsibility is 'to be'—to be for others and for you, Lord. Like the times at table, when eating is the thing, savouring the nourishment and delighting the spiritual taste buds till I'm glad to be alive and the rest of the 'family' around me are grateful for my life also. Should this be any different at the table of the Lord?

Please let me dip in the bowl with you, Lord, whether the taste be bitter or sweet. Amen

Saturday

THE CUP

While they were eating, he took a loaf of bread, and after blessing it he broke it, gave it to them, and said, 'Take; this is my body.' Then he took a cup, and after giving thanks he gave it to them, and all of them drank from it. He said to them, 'This is my blood of the covenant, which is poured out for many. Truly I tell you, I will never again drink of the fruit of the vine until that day when I drink it new in the kingdom of God.'
MARK 14:22–25

At first she did not recognize the goblet from her dream. Its simplicity belied its importance. It was no different from the others in the set, arranged around the table for every man to drink from. Nothing would have distinguished it in the washing-up bowl, but one thing placed it apart for her. At this moment it rested, firmly cupped, in her Master's hands.

Jesus had already blessed the bread as every Jew would have done before passing it to the hungry family. She hardly noticed the words he had spoken over the bread, everyone was chatting and enjoying the meal so much—although one or two glanced round slightly surprised when he said, 'This is my body.' They did not expect such a phrase in a traditional Passover feast. Still, Jesus was always more of a poet than most, and they had learnt to permit him licence. It was when he said, 'This is my blood' at the raising of the wine that a hush fell over the room. 'This is my blood of the covenant, which is poured out for many,' she heard him say clearly. Now that certainly had no part in the Passover wording.

Up until this day, each of the four cups at Passover had represented a promise of the Father to his chosen people—a promise of freedom, of deliverance, of redemption, a promise of an irrefutable relationship between God and his people. If 'blood' entered the language of this feast at all, it would have been in the context of the blood sprinkled on the doorposts of the Israelites during their preparation for escape from Egypt, and that blood was the blood of a sacrificial lamb slain for the deliverance of the people. No wonder faces looked puzzled. How could this cup relate to Jesus? How could he say, 'This is my blood'? She wished she could discern individual conversations in the low, reverent chatter that evolved during the meal. Now and then the odd comment reached her ears. Someone whispered something about comments Jesus had made previously on his ministry travels, about his death. Others talked about the role of a Messiah. Others debated the niceties of various elements of the Passover feast itself, and there were others who relaxed and made pleasant conversation with their neighbours, as you do at family meals. From where she was sitting she could not see John's face, obscured as it was by the eager attentions of the servants as they bobbed and darted back and forth to replenish the food and remove the dirty dishes. She guessed that he was silent; she imagined that tears of bereavement would already be shining in his eyes. He stayed close to the side of his beloved Jesus throughout the meal.

Looking slowly around the room, the traveller felt a great sadness envelop her as she identified so many parallels to the 'feasting' of this sacrament in the many denominations of the Church at home, in her century. She thought of the 'babble' the people of her time made of such a simple sharing of bread and wine. This intimate family meal among trusted friends was now often an issue for controversy and debate—how it should be conducted, who administers the sacrament, the true theological meaning of the act of communion itself, the nature, size, shape and content of the elements, all debatable. Even the piece of furniture that the meal rested upon, the table, had in some denominations become 'sacred' to the extent that no one dared move it six inches to the right or left without a committee first giving permission. Will the numerous denominations ever stop the 'babble' and focus on Christ? she wondered; and she prayed, 'Please enable us to look up from our individual overflowing plates and attend to his words, his actions, his presence.'

As the goblet of wine that Jesus had blessed continued to be passed around the room for each disciple to drink, Trav's eyes followed its progress in awe—not mesmerized by the cup itself but fascinated by the future esteem and mystique that would be afforded this simple piece of tableware. Here it was—the legendary 'Holy Grail', around which generations to come would spin grand tales of deeds and misdeeds and make film producers rich on the takings. How casually the disciples handled it; how insignificant it appeared amid the trappings of first-century Palestine. The thought then struck her forcefully: but was that not exactly how Jesus himself was being treated? Just another holy man among so many, one more good rabbi for the learning—and soon it would be one more criminal for a cross. How she would have loved to take that goblet home and show it to the world; to say, 'Look, here is your cherished object, but the power is not in it but in the living Christ.' She longed to be seen by him, as in her dream; to handle the cup and hold it before his eyes, saying, 'Take my life, Lord, use me as you use this cup, a willing instument in your service.' He knows, she comforted herself. At home, in the 21st century, he knows all that I would say to him. 'Thank you, Lord,' she prayed, 'thank you that you are waiting for me on my return.'

Yet here, in an upper room in Jerusalem, the Lord of the universe was gently and patiently attempting to bring men whom he had trained for three years to a deeper understanding of his mission to the earth and of their God-appointed task when he would leave them. How blind many of them were, and how preoccupied with their own concerns. The traveller knew now why she felt at home with this little band, despite her previous hesitancy on entering the room. In them she recognized familiar attitudes inherent in her generation.

Jesus was still there. His smile was being offered to all around that table, his hands working overtime to pour and to reach and to pass around the food and drink, making sure that no one went without. He knows, she thought, and the realization staggered her. He knows how much or how little they understand, how far they are from fully comprehending what he is about to do, and he has not left the room. Not here in Palestine, two thousand years ago, nor in the hallowed portals of the many and varied gatherings of his body in her times would he ever leave the feast—no, not until all the hungry souls were filled.

Dear Lord, forgive our lack of understanding, and all the mixed motives that bring people to your feast. Someday, in your perfect kingdom beyond this world, our feasting will satisfy as you intended it to do, pure and undefiled. Meantime, we go hungry if we stay away. Draw us to your table; help us to celebrate. Amen

CHOICES

Sunday

THE SERVANT KING

After he had washed their feet, had put on his robe, and had returned to the table, he said to them, 'Do you know what I have done to you? You call me Teacher and Lord—and you are right, for that is what I am. So if I, your Lord and Teacher, have washed your feet, you also ought to wash one another's feet. For I have set you an example, that you also should do as I have done to you. Very truly, I tell you, servants are not greater than their master; nor are messengers greater than the one who sent them. If you know these things, you are blessed if you do them.'

JOHN 13:12–17 (READ ALSO VV. 1–11)

It was difficult for her to watch the actions of Jesus after the supper. She had felt more comfortable observing Mary anointing Jesus' feet and drying them with her hair. But seeing that towel and basin in Christ's hands— those same objects she had seen in her dream—watching him bend low upon the floor, each pair of disciple's feet cupped in his hands as he washed the grime and dirt of the journey from their skin, made her hackles rise. What was wrong? Hadn't the servants done their job properly when the disciples had arrived for the special feast? It was a routine task upon entry of every home to cleanse the feet, and she appreciated the necessity even more now that she had trodden those grime-laden, dusty dirt-tracks around the countryside. Even with her 21st-century hiking boots, a foot-bath would have been more than welcome. She imagined how much more the natives of this century would welcome it, wearing only rough, open sandals. Surely it would have been all the more essential as part of the purification rituals for such a feast, to wash before eating.

Yet here was Jesus 'doing the needful' after supper. Maybe he was trying to make a point. What a surprise for the servants to see the chief guest in the house, the one who had booked the room, who in this gathering acted as the host would act throughout the feast, now doing their job with basin and towel.

Just as the traveller had not attempted to touch the cup in Christ's hands, knowing that she was no longer dreaming and could not effect change anyway, so also she restrained herself from attempting to pick up the towel and basin. She wished she could, though. She would gladly have saved her Master from this menial task. He had better things to do, she reckoned. Peter seemed to think so also. He even protested, not realizing that only Jesus could fully cleanse him and enable him to enter into full fellowship and relationship with himself, the Christ. Poor Simon, she thought—so brash, so earnest, his sincerity transparent as he gets the idea and volunteers for the full works without comprehending the symbolism of what Jesus was demonstrating. This act of love, on Jesus' part, in its unreserved caring, its ignoring of all preference of worldly status, its parallel with the cleansing power of what Jesus would do at Calvary, scared her. If Peter had got it wrong, how much more might she be missing the point?

Suddenly a premonition flashed before her mind—the visual image of what she knew, from scripture, lay ahead. She saw another towel and basin similar to this one, but the hands that held it were different. They were cultured hands, not used to manual labour—no carpenter, this. He wore rich robes of bright and costly material and as he dipped his hands deep into the water in a feeble attempt to cleanse his soul from guilt, she heard Pilate say, 'I am innocent of this man's blood. See to it yourselves' (Matthew 27:24).

In the upper room, she wished she were still in her dream, able to grasp that basin from Jesus' hands and show him how Pilate would soon try to wash the Lord's blood from his conscience. She wished she could cry out to Jesus, 'Tell him, tell Pilate you are innocent. He is open to the truth. Make a defence and Pilate will let you go free. He knows you have done no wrong.' But even as these desires overwhelmed her, she saw a goblet lying accidentally overturned upon the floor, and as the rich red wine spilt its blood-red stain across the floor, Trav knew beyond all question that she could not, dared not, stop the spilling of God's blood, or she herself would have to cleanse her hands of the deed. The world was waiting, desperately waiting for salvation. Instead she held invisible hands out towards the towel and basin, praying with tears in her eyes, 'Wash me too, Lord, wash me clean.'

Where might she have to stoop to acknowledge that she was not greater than her master? What would the showing of love yet cost her in his service? Could she journey all the way to Calvary?

'If only the world was not so needy, Lord,' she prayed silently. 'There are too many people in my world at home—hurting souls, bent double with sorrows. You hear the cries of the lost ones, who don't know your saving power; the bereaved ones whose days are dark with grief; the ignorant ones who believe that life in the absence of you is all the happiness there is; the despairing ones whose living no longer embraces hope; those laid low with burdens of sickness or handicap or failure, or self-esteem fractured by abuse or rejection or desertion or betrayal or... Oh no, Lord, there are too many people. I cannot help them all. I am only one person...'

She broke off her prayer because someone was leaving the banquet. One of the disciples had quietly and discreetly risen to his feet and was, even as she looked around, stepping out through the door. Only by the conversation of the others did she ascertain whom Jesus had asked to leave. The disciples were chatting about his departure. One wondered, 'Where is Judas off to?' Another guessed that he was away on an errand, as he was the treasurer of the group. Maybe Jesus had sent out for more food, or to send a donation to one of the many charities thronging the marketplace, but nobody was sure, no one really knew why he had gone, although, since Jesus himself had sent him, they reckoned it was none of their business.

None of their business, thought the traveller! There were eleven left and only one of Judas. If only they had taken some responsibility, rather than leaving everything to be 'sorted' by Jesus. If only they'd asked the right questions, followed up on the hints Jesus had dropped during supper, even cared enough to volunteer to go out with Judas as his colleagues.

Dear Lord, the responsibility is ours, isn't it? Not the blame for all the world's ills or the task to solve every one of them, but the privilege, the honour of seeing the difference your salvation makes for a broken world when our efforts of action, sacrificial use of time, finance, and love, are supplied to the circumstances in which our day-to-day lives are rooted. I can't stop the earthquakes, Lord, or the famines or the terrorism, and no volcano's power is mine to quench, but you put me on this planet for a reason. You gave me your salvation and hope for a task. Help me to take responsibility for what is at my hand. Bring me some feet to wash today. Amen

Monday

MOUNTAIN ASPIRATIONS

When they had sung the hymn, they went out to the Mount of Olives. And Jesus said to them, 'You will all become deserters; for it is written, "I will strike the shepherd, and the sheep will be scattered." But after I am raised up, I will go before you to Galilee.' Peter said to him, 'Even though all become deserters, I will not.' Jesus said to him, 'Truly I tell you, this day, this very night, before the cock crows twice, you will deny me three times.' But he said vehemently, 'Even though I must die with you, I will not deny you.' And all of them said the same.

MARK 14:26–31

It wasn't a difficult climb, following Jesus and his disciples to the Mount of Olives. It wasn't a high hill at all, not compared to the Alps, or even some of the lesser mountains where the traveller lived—more of a pleasant incline, really, to the top of the grassy mound. But what a height it represented in terms of the cultural memories of the locals! It had been a focal point of worship for the Jews since King David's day (2 Samuel 15:30) and held a powerful association with the Lord's coming even from the days of Zechariah (Zechariah 14:4). It was also a sanctuary in the heart of Jesus and his disciples, where they would withdraw from the pressures of ministry and from where Jesus prepared to make his entry of triumph to Jerusalem. From this Mount he was able to teach his disciples many things in secret. Later, she recalled, Jesus would choose this very hillock from which to ascend into heaven. Not a slope to be sneezed at, she mused.

What a place for Jesus to choose to break the news to Peter of his forthcoming failure. What a location for all the disciples to learn how futile their good intentions would prove to be when it came to the crunch. But then wasn't it Zechariah again who had prophesied the strike upon the Shepherd that would scatter the sheep? (Zechariah 13:7). With so many of the pieces of the jigsaw falling into place, how could they have been so blind? she wondered. How many hints did they need for this crossword puzzle?

They were not engaged in puzzle solving for fun, though. This was real life, and they were living right in the centre of it, putting it together piece by crazy piece. They only had a moment-by-moment experience of what was happening and could not see the big picture with the benefit of hindsight.

At that time, Peter's declaration of his own loyalty was stronger in his mind than the warnings from his Lord. The disciples were having another 'mountain-top experience' on Mount Olivet and nothing could bring them down to earth. If only Paul had already written his famous letter to the Romans pointing out the conundrum that we cannot do the good things we most want to do (Romans 7:15–20). Then they might have understood a little better that all the very best intentions in the world, all the gargantuan efforts on their part to do right, would still end in tears. That's why Jesus had to come.

She sighed, wishing that the history of the world in her own time had proved this wrong. After all, a single generation had witnessed the space race to the moon, the triumph of organ transplants, the successful battle against many previously deadly diseases, the mapping of the human genome, to name only a few victorious steps of positive progress in human development. Yet hospitals, schools and homes were no longer guaranteed places of safety. Less and less respect was shown for authority, property or peace, and terrorism held to ransom many great nations. All the affluence in the world had not produced universal sharing of resources to the point of obliterating poverty and famine. All the scientific resources and technology in the world had so far failed to solve the curse at the centre of the problem—the problem of the human heart.

It was a reasonable view from the summit of the Mount of Olives, yet the disciples could not see into the depths of their own hearts. Time and time again during these final days of his physical dwelling upon earth,

Jesus tried to warn them, to alert them, to prepare them so that they could guard themselves against the acts of betrayal, denial and desertion that they would soon perpetrate against him.

Trav settled down upon a cold stone and remembered what the Bible said Judas had planned and was in the process of executing right now. 'Oh, DC,' she moaned, 'I'd have paid him much more than that *not* to do it.' She didn't really expect the dream carrier to appear just then, but, as if he had been awaiting her call, there he was perched on a nearby rock.

'Come on!' he ordered, but there was a lightness in his tone.

'Where are we going? Wait, the others are on their way down this hill. I don't want to lose them.'

'You won't lose them, Trav,' he sang out as he pulled her in the opposite direction. 'Besides, they're on their way down for a rest in a nice quiet garden. They'll be there most of the night. You can catch up later. We've got a bit of horticulture to do ourselves, girl. Look, another garden!'

Suddenly, as if borne on the air, they both landed in an unfamiliar place and DC began his story.

'It was thousands of years ago when I carried my first dream. I wouldn't like to tell you how long exactly—makes me feel old. But she was so beautiful, the lady, living with Adam in this lovely garden. Eden, they called it then. She really enjoyed the dream about animals and plants and her becoming the mother of all human children. When she wasn't dreaming about the way the garden could develop and grow, she enjoyed great chats with the Boss—and walks, the three of them had great walks together, planning the future.

'Then another dreamer got to her, and he was a real snake in the grass. He told her a lot of lies and made her doubt the plans the Boss had for her. She thought she could do better...'

The traveller stopped him there, mid-flow. 'Eve. You're talking about Eve, aren't you, DC? Well, I know the story, and it has too sad an ending for the way I feel today.'

'Is that right, Trav? You think the story has an ending, do you?'

She was slowly making her way through avenues of heavily laden fruit trees, trying to avoid snagging her ankles in the matted undergrowth under her feet. 'It's all in a mess now, DC. This place hasn't been taken care of, not like the Boss meant it to be.'

DC was chomping on a ripe piece of fruit. 'Good harvest though, girl. Pretty abundant, wouldn't you say?'

'That's no thanks to Adam or Eve, is it?'

'Exactly.' He swung round on his heels and looked straight at her, with a serious expression on his face. 'They made a wrong decision, they messed up pretty badly—with the earth, the livestock, the natural resources, the children—but he,' stabbing his thumb at the sky, '*he* is still in control of the harvest.'

'You mean it's not over yet?'

'Not by a long chalk, Trav. They only got to insert the commas and full stops; *he* writes the book.'

'Couldn't he have taken care of the punctuation too, DC? That might have saved a lot of trouble down through the centuries.'

'Yeah, but what part would they have played in the conversation then, Trav? God doesn't go around talking to himself. This whole creation thing is about relationship. How was he going to develop a meaningful relationship with creatures who had no say in the matter?'

'So he gave them a say, and Judas a say, and he won't take that away from us, no matter how much we mess up the situation?'

'You got it, traveller,' and DC was grinning at her now. 'Until the end.'

Dear Creator God, on my walk to Calvary, open my eyes to the decisions you want me to make. When temptation deflects or exhaustion slows me down, or stupidity hinders or pride distorts my path, walk with me and grow only the harvest you have designed for my gathering. Amen

Tuesday

THE CHOICE

They went to a place called Gethsemane; and he said to his disciples, 'Sit here while I pray.' He took with him Peter and James and John, and began to be distressed and agitated. And he said to them, 'I am deeply grieved, even to death; remain here, and keep awake.' And going a little farther, he threw himself on the ground and prayed that, if it were possible, the hour might pass from him. He said, 'Abba, Father, for you all things are possible; remove this cup from me; yet, not what I want, but what you want.' He came and found them sleeping; and he said to Peter, 'Simon, are you asleep? Could you not keep awake one hour? Keep awake and pray that you may not come into the time of trial; the spirit indeed is willing, but the flesh is weak.' And again he went away and prayed, saying the same words. And once more he came and found them sleeping, for their eyes were very heavy; and they did not know what to say to him. He came a third time and said to them, 'Are you still sleeping and taking your rest? Enough! The hour has come; the Son of Man is betrayed into the hands of sinners. Get up, let us be going. See, my betrayer is at hand.'

MARK 14:32–42

The one garden seemed almost to merge into the other as DC returned Trav instantly to where the disciples had walked a short distance from the summit of Mount Olivet. The garden of Gethsemane grew olives, lots of them, the sturdy stumpy trees spreading their canopy along neat avenues on a hill overlooking the city. What a view, she thought as the candle-lit city blinked through the darkness, but the disciples weren't admiring the view. This also was a familiar place to them where Jesus often brought them to pray, to relax and to learn. They felt safe here: it was their 'retreat'. It had been a wonderful supper and the meal settled warmly in their stomachs. Lulled into a false sense of security by the familiar surroundings, their full stomachs, and the nearness of their Master, it was no wonder, as deeper darkness threw its cover over the garden, that they fell asleep.

She passed the majority of the disciples, out for the count beneath the olive trees. Walking on a little further, she found three more, Peter, James and John, on guard, scanning the path that wound its thin ribbon down into the city where Judas had gone, each one taking turns to pray while the other two kept watch. Peter was determined not to be caught off guard: he had even brought a sword with him to the garden. Jesus was not with them.

Now she knew where she would find him. Whatever other parts of the Bible she might have missed, forgotten or skipped over, the part that told of Gethsemane was not one of them. She knew well that, just a stone's throw away, he would be there, leaning in emotional exhaustion against an old olive tree, sinking in devastation to his knees, his tears falling like drops of blood on to the ground (Luke 22:44), and she could not move closer. She knew how her heart had been wrenched, watching him weep at the grave of Lazarus, and this... this she could not bear. She stayed with the three disciples, watching them, who had been so determined to keep watch for Jesus, all slowly sinking into sleep, every one of them—even Peter, who had sworn to die with him if necessary. It was enough for her; she could bear no more. She went no further but sat upon the ground with the disciples, sobbing tears as invisible to them as she herself was, imagining her Lord in his anguish. He must be begging his Father to find another way, pleading to be spared the incredible horror that lay ahead for him, and yet she felt his strength. Even though the trees hid him from her view, she was aware of a deep sense of resolve, an atmosphere of love and devotion that was almost tangible, even at this distance. 'Father,' she prayed, 'it must be you. You are here. Oh thank you, thank you that you are here.'

Suddenly something changed. She could not tell what, or how it happened, but there was a change of consistency in the air around her—the darkness seemed less heavy, the air less thick with sorrow—and she knew her Lord must have spoken those amazing words, 'Yet not what I will, but what thou wilt.' The co-creator of the universe had submitted to the Father's will and the earth would be saved. She knew then that if God had not forced Adam or Eve to obey him against their will, he would not force Jesus, or, for that matter, herself.

What a frightening thought that was. It meant that she could choose to live without him, to find happiness of a kind outside his will, to accept second best for her life, to chase dreams he never sent, select options he'd never designed, spend an eternity where he was not. The choice was hers, hers alone, and how terrifying was that, she wondered, for the citizens of her century, many of whom took it all for granted, expecting the Boss to carry them to safety while they slept in apathy, ignorant of the choice they must make.

'Wake up!' she screamed, shaking Peter's shoulder. 'Wake up James, get John to his feet! Look, look, the Lord is coming, he's coming.' But they did not hear her; they slept on as Jesus, haggard and pale with weeping, eyes red-rimmed, came slowly to their side. She felt the stab of pain in her own heart at his disappointment to find them sleeping. She heard his words, 'Watch and pray that you may not enter into temptation' and she remembered the number of times she had dozed off during her daily quiet times at home. She determined to choose a different period of the day to concentrate on lengthy prayer, not when she was likely to fall asleep in exhaustion. To make quality time for Jesus was the least she could do.

As he repeated the exercise not once but twice more—alerting them, leaving them; returning, alerting them, leaving them; and then finding them asleep a third time—she felt ashamed, ashamed of the countless warnings believers in her time had already received against ignoring his commands. From the Bible, the Church, even from our own experiences, Christ calls to us loudly and with clarity and still we sleep on, refusing to arm ourselves against evil, to claim victory in spiritual warfare. She couldn't help wondering how different the road to Calvary might have been for those disciples if they had watched with him one hour in prayer that night. But now it was too late. A group of people were entering the garden—a rabble with swords and clubs—and Jesus knew they were coming for him.

Dear Lord, forgive every heedless moment I choose to live outside your will. Let me not desert you when the battle with the Bad 'Un is subtly waged. Show me where the 'front line' is for me, at home, at work, and when I relax. Amen

Wednesday

A KIND OF LOVING

Immediately, while he was still speaking, Judas, one of the twelve, arrived; and with him there was a crowd with swords and clubs, from the chief priests, the scribes, and the elders. Now the betrayer had given them a sign, saying, 'The one I will kiss is the man; arrest him and lead him away under guard.' So when he came, he went up to him at once and said, 'Rabbi!' and kissed him. Then they laid hands on him and arrested him. But one of those who stood near drew his sword and struck the slave of the high priest, cutting off his ear. Then Jesus said to them, 'Have you come out with swords and clubs to arrest me as though I were a bandit? Day after day I was with you in the temple teaching, and you did not arrest me. But let the scriptures be fulfilled.' All of them deserted him and fled.

MARK 14:43–50

How many times had Jesus given them the sign of peace? During Passover, at sabbath worship, visiting in the home at Bethany, when walking through the cornfields, sailing across Galilee, preaching to crowds on a hilltop? How many times? She could only guess. How often was it used in her church at home?

In her time it usually took the form of a religious benediction spoken formally by the minister. Sometimes, in less formal worship, the congregation would be invited to turn to one another and, smiling, hand clasped around hand, all four hands involved in the embrace, each pair of worshippers would express their bond of peace and fellowship. However it was done, it was meant to be a love sign, Christian to Christian, and God to his children.

The gesture that Judas chose to signal who Jesus was, in order to betray him, was the self-same gesture of love and devotion used by any disciple when he greeted his rabbi. It was a kiss that signalled submission to the superior position of the rabbi, a sign of homage. So when Judas used it this time, it signalled only a lie. Rather than bowing the knee, Judas was, by this sign, betraying his master.

She wished she could see inside this disciple's head. By what crazy 'double-speak' had he talked himself into this act of treachery? Surely it couldn't have been for the money: he soon discarded his payment of thirty silver pieces. Did some misunderstood, perverted religious or political agenda push Judas to test Christ's hand, attempting to force him to 'bring in the kingdom' immediately? Did he actually think he was helping Christ, judging the progression of the events of that critical week by his own feeble human standards? There was no way for the traveller to be able to answer her own questions, only the Boss himself knew the thoughts in the heart of Judas. It was a salutary reminder to her, though, of how any individual, pushed to the limits of their own thinking and standards, could justify anything to themselves, as regards their own actions at any given point in their journey to Calvary.

How many acts of religious intolerance have sheltered under the flag of patriotism? she thought. How many acts of violence, by bomb or law or tongue, sheltered behind a shield of genuine religious zeal? How many times does fear, greed or impatience for a final solution to an unresolved and critical problem push otherwise decent people towards the very edge of the precipice of their own convictions? How many allow that pressure to push them over the cliff?

In Judas' hands that evening, the future salvation of the world did not lie. In his hands lay only a decision about what kind of loving he would show to the one who already loved him unconditionally. The kiss of a disciple for his master is indeed a special kind of loving. Judas did not merely twist it that night, but betrayed the relationship with his Lord built up over the preceding three years. Trav's thoughts ran on: if the relationship with Jesus means anything, it has to mean trust—trust that Christ really does know best what he is about in our lives, even if the circumstances in which we find ourselves are shot to pieces and we don't know why. The relationship has to mean love, not merely the outward gestures of dutiful religious observance and practice, like Judas' kiss, but the daily inner sacrifice of body, will and soul in that hard trek all the way to Calvary. It means the joy of doing the Master's will because we feel his pleasure affirming our actions. What pleasure did Judas feel that night when he heard Jesus say the words, 'Judas, is it with a kiss that you are betraying the Son of Man?' (Luke 22:48). The traveller could not clearly see the look exchanged between the two dramatic figures, standing face to face in the darkness, but she knew that the subsequent actions of the betrayer would be eloquent enough testimony of the innocence he saw in Jesus' face (Matthew 27:3–5).

Remembering her dream, Trav imagined herself picking up those thirty pieces of silver, gathering them slowly, piece by tainted piece, and laying them before the chief priests to ask, 'Is this the price you would put on the Messiah's head?' But then she would have been preaching to the converted, for weren't they already aware of the implications of the betrayal? (Matthew 27:6). But the chief priests, taking the pieces of silver, had said, 'It is not lawful to put them into the treasury, since they are blood money.' She could not discern a sense of remorse in what she read in the Gospels. There was only an obsessive desire to keep the law and not to taint the treasury, and no desire at all to open their minds to the possibility of a startling new truth. The very Saviour whose coming heralded the fulfilment of the law itself was sold for a pittance and their concern was rather for the unsullied nature of the treasury. The law could not fault these zealous religious leaders. No wonder Jesus had to come.

Trav longed to tell them about the mercy, love and justice that would be executed for all time at Calvary. It was a cautionary tale indeed for the Church of every age. She could not make a difference to the situation in Palestine just then; but Trav knew that she must return soon to the modern Church, and there her resolve to help change things for the kingdom of God would be tested.

Strange, she mused, that it should be Judas himself whom God permitted to testify to Jesus' innocence within the very stronghold of the enemy, at a time when that powerful committee of chief priests and elders were meeting to seal the final plans for his death (Matthew 27:4). Was it one last chance for those 'holy men' to see the error of their ways? But they would reject the opportunity and the die would be cast, not only for Judas, but also for themselves.

Suddenly she was jolted back to the events right there in the garden of Gethsemane. Peter was proving his allegiance to the Prince of Peace by lashing out and cutting off the ear of the high priest's slave. Trav cast her mind back to the upper room when, following the supper, Jesus had tried to prepare the disciples for their impending trauma (Luke 22:31–38). As they appeared to be unaware of how close they were to the moment of ultimate danger, Jesus employed some pretty drastic shock tactics. He appeared to contradict some of his previous teaching about not relying upon worldly means for their survival—'no purse, no bag, no sandals' (Luke 10:4)—and told them to equip themselves with these very items, as well as a sword. Trav wondered if Jesus was trying to shake them from their complacency. In preparing them for the bereavement ahead, he was recalling to their minds the world's false security and their own vulnerability. As Jesus was not in the business of contradicting himself, Trav imagined that he meant his words not to be taken literally, but the upshot of his attempt to alert them was that this went completely over their heads. Unfortunately, they did take his comments quite literally. 'Look, Lord,' they said, 'here are two swords.'

Trav could imagine what a long sigh Jesus might justifiably have made at this sugggestion. He must have realized at this point that they still had not got the message. Patiently he dismissed their suggestion with casual indifference: 'It is enough,' he said.

What a long-suffering teacher he was, and what great wisdom he employed, she thought. He waited to the very moment of his arrest to make his point literally, on the edge of the sword thrust itself. His understanding of the human mind was faultless. Trav discerned that this was one object lesson that Peter would never forget, for, sword in hand, blood dripping from the servant's ear, with his Master's reprimand ringing in his ears, the experience would have imprinted itself on that disciple's mind for ever.

'Please, come home with me, Lord,' Trav prayed. 'Work your patient teaching there—on the riotous streets of urban English cities, where black and white wield knives of hate; on the devastated streets of Ulster where bomb and bullet and decades of terrorism hold your truth hostage to fear; and amid the dark traffic of modern minds where purse and bag, sandal and the equivalent of the sword still vie with the desire to trust only in you.' If she had still been within her dream, she would have taken that sword and attempted to break it across her knee long before the supper had ended. But then, would Peter have properly learnt his lesson for life? And what about that other sword? According to scripture, there were two swords mentioned that night. The second one must not have been used, as it was never mentioned again. Someone got the message, after all.

Mark's Gospel, she knew, made little of Peter's mistake (Mark 14:47), but John would not only tell us that Peter was the culprit; he would give the very name of the slave (John 18:10). She had sometimes wondered whether he had stayed close enough to Jesus to do a little 'follow up' on the healing that Christ performed immediately to the wounded ear. Certainly the other disciples did not. When they realized that Jesus was forbidding them to use physical violence in his defence, they could imagine no other way of helping him, and they fled.

Dear Master, grant me a holy imagination—the ability to discover ways and means of solving problems that do not utilize the ways and means of the world. You showed so clearly by your life and ministry that the end cannot be made to justify the means.

But Lord, the alternative solution might cost me dearly. What would imprisonment have meant to the disciples if they had stayed with Jesus in the garden? Give me courage; help me to stay. Amen

Thursday

ODDS AGAINST

A certain young man was following him, wearing nothing but a linen cloth. They caught hold of him, but he left the linen cloth and ran off naked.

They took Jesus to the high priest; and all the chief priests, the elders, and the scribes were assembled. Peter had followed him at a distance, right into the courtyard of the high priest; and he was sitting with the guards, warming himself at the fire.

MARK 14:51–54 (READ ALSO VV. 55–72)

The traveller smiled as the young man raced away, leaving his linen robe behind him. At least he had shown the bravery to continue alone in Christ's footsteps as the Lord was led from the garden as a prisoner. The lad had the ingenuity to slip out of his slim garment when he also was grabbed by the mob, and he ran for his life, naked but free.

Had he intended to come so close to being arrested? Did he with youthful bravado dream of sharing the danger with Christ all the way to Calvary? Did he imagine that he could glean enough information 'under cover' to report back to the others? Or did the brashness of youth blind him to the dangers? Who was he, anyway? She couldn't quite see. If Mark alone had recorded the event in his Gospel, it must have been more significant to him than to the other writers. Maybe he had a personal investment in the memory. Perhaps it was young Mark himself who had fled naked from the scene, having followed Jesus longer than the others?

Was this, she wondered, a well-respected Gospel writer's plaintive attempt to say, 'I tried, I really tried'? Writing his account of the events of that historic week as a mature and established missionary and leader of the early Christian Church, did Mark still carry with him the frustration of that feeling of utter helplessness in the face of insurmountable odds which must have haunted the young lad as he ran?

If he had felt like this, how much more frightened must the other disciples have been? And here was Peter, she thought, still smarting from Jesus' rebuke and command to put up his sword, yet still following wherever his discipleship would lead, right into the lions' den. No wonder the Lord entrusted the leadership of the Church into this man's hands. But first, Peter had to learn an important lesson. First, this strong man, this big fisherman, well used to physical labour and winning through by the power of his muscles, had to feel what it was like to be in the ultimate 'odds against' situation, without redress to his sword.

At that moment, in the courtyard of the enemy, how was he feeling? Like Gideon, about to face the Midianites with a reduced army, much too small for the task? Like Samson, without the strength his hair had once afforded him? Like Jonah, trapped in the belly of the whale? A mere stone's throw from him, across the courtyard, the divine power that helped to create a universe stood in chains awaiting trial. And all Peter could feel was fear.

The traveller had followed Peter into the courtyard, and stayed with him there. She had no desire to hear the falsehoods spoken by witness after witness at the mockery of a trial that was now getting under way. No two witnesses were able to agree on their fabricated stories, so the lawyers could make nothing stick according to the Old Testament law. In an attempt to make the defendant incriminate himself, the high priest was questioning Jesus about his own nature: 'Are you the Messiah, the Son of the Blessed One?' In contrast to his previous silent refusal to defend himself or to incriminate the false witnesses, Jesus replied, 'I am.'

The traveller heard none of this, but the cheers of victory that emanated from the court as the high priest tore his garments in ritual mourning at the sound of what he considered to be blasphemy from the lips of Jesus were clearly heard by Peter and the others warming themselves by the fire outside. The disciple's face was ashen. It was obvious that the high priest had secured evidence enough from the Lord's own lips to proclaim a verdict. But what the Jews could not do at this point was to secure a sentence or proceed with an execution. That lay with an authority and a court higher than theirs. The Roman authorities would have to become involved.

She wondered if, even at this point in the proceedings, Peter desperately hoped that there would be a way out—something he could do with those strong muscles, a way to set Jesus free. The jeers of the bribed witnesses, the insults of the 'rent-a-crowd' at this false trial, mocking Jesus with shouts of 'Prophesy!' and the sound of the guards raining down blows upon him as they moved him out of the courtroom, all were clearly heard in the courtyard, and beads of perspiration began to run slowly down Peter's forehead.

The maid perhaps thought he looked a bit odd, huddled there, close to the fire, his cloak pulled tightly around his face, intent upon warming himself further despite the beads of sweat upon his brow. 'Were you with him?' she queried. It was unnerving for Peter. A challenge from one of the men he could have coped with, even from a guard. A strong right hook would have taken care of it. But the maid of the high priest, what was he supposed to do with her? Denial and flight seemed the only form of self-defence open to him.

Still the maid pursued him to the gateway, where a crowd often lingered to catch the gossip after a juicy trial. She kept asking their opinion, and they glanced at his clothes and heard his accent as he denied the charge a second time. But still Peter did not leave. After a while, the whole crowd began to accuse him. 'You are a Galilean,' they shouted, a little too loudly for comfort. The guards were in the process of leading a prisoner across the courtyard now and if he didn't do something quickly the growing interest of the crowd would attract their attention. In desperation he swore that he did not know Jesus. For a second time a cock crowed and, remembering the words of the Lord (Mark 14:30), Peter dared not even glance up to see what prisoner was even now watching him across the courtyard.

The traveller did not know whom to feel for the most at that moment— a failed disciple, broken and weeping tears of deep repentance as he fled to the safety of home, or an innocent prisoner in chains being roughly pulled to his cell, the spit of scoundrels running down his face and the echo of his chief follower's voice, in denial of their very aquaintance, ringing in his ears.

Dear Lord, it must have been horrific. Pain is pain and the body breaks with it. Torture is brutal and the mind weakens under the strain. But betrayal, that's by far the worst, for it crucifies the heart.

Judas began the sword thrust, but Peter's denial must have turned the blade in an open wound, and what is more painful than that?

He didn't mean to be cruel—he was so scared—and I thank you that you forgave him, Lord. Forgive us, your followers, when our fear betrays you daily. Amen

Friday

TRUTH'S SHADOW

As soon as it was morning, the chief priests held a consultation with the elders and scribes and the whole council. They bound Jesus, led him away, and handed him over to Pilate. Pilate asked him, 'Are you the King of the Jews?' He answered him, 'You say so.' Then the chief priests accused him of many things. Pilate asked him again, 'Have you no answer? See how many charges they bring against you.' But Jesus made no further reply, so that Pilate was amazed.

MARK 15:1–5 (READ ALSO VV. 6–20)

Standing before the Roman procurator, Jesus looked even more vulnerable than before the Jews—at least, it seemed so to the traveller. After all, they were his own people, of his nation and religion, his kith and kin, and she had imagined he might stand some chance with them. Here the whole weight of the Roman empire was aligned against him—an empire that cared little for the Jews or their God.

But the strangest process of law was taking place in this second court-room and she could hardly fathom what was going on. Many accusations were levelled at Jesus, from political treason to tax evasion (Luke 23:1–2), and the amazing thing was that Pilate believed none of it. Was this official of the Roman government genuinely trying to get at the truth? It wasn't until the elders and chief priests and scribes insisted that Jesus was making a claim to kingship of the nation of Judea that Pilate took notice. After all, the empire had to be protected at all costs from a local uprising.

She watched the stately procurator look into Christ's eyes and put the question to him directly: 'Are you the King of the Jews?' There was something in Pilate's eyes then—was it fear, or genuine integrity and respect for his own law? she wondered. Did the shadow of truth fall, even then, across Pilate's heart as he tried to goad the Lord into building a case for his own defence? Jesus remained silent and Pilate's mind was still undecided.

'She told him, you know,' came DC's voice from a bench behind. The traveller turned to face the dream carrier, her eyebrows raised in question. 'Pilate,' he said, stabbing a thumb to the front of the court, 'he had due warning from his Mrs, I carried the dream to her myself. Look, here comes her messenger now.'

Sure enough, a slave had been admitted to the courtroom and was hastily delivering a message to Pilate. All judgment halted while he took note of his wife's warning. Trav knew the words from Mathew 27 very well: 'Have nothing to do with that innocent man…'. She held her breath. This could be it, she thought. This could be the moment when Pilate resists the fears for his future, his position, his livelihood, and allows truth—the truth he knows, for he fully realizes that the priests' chief motivation for bringing the prisoner to him is envy (v. 18)—allows that truth to direct his actions and set Jesus free.

Desperately, Pilate grabbed at a straw. Tradition allowed him to be merciful to one prisoner during this period of annual feasting. Swinging the weight of the court into action, he offered the gathered crowd a choice of prisoner to be set free, pitting Jesus against a criminal called Barabbas.

DC muttered his own comments on Pilate's merciful offer. 'He's proud of this tradition, you know. He thinks it secures his popularity with the people—well, perhaps not popularity exactly, but something less than hatred. This choice between Jesus and a common criminal, Pilate imagines, should get him out of trouble. "No contest," he thinks. "Jesus, the popular hero, flavour of the month with lepers and lawyers alike, healer, teacher, all-round good egg—no problem, it's as good as done." Besides, he imagines he won't be to blame if something goes wrong. But something's going badly wrong with his plan, all right! He's tried to manipulate the situation, to procure the honest outcome while hanging on to his own popularity and position. But he can't have his cake and eat it too. See, Trav? Pilate's a bit too sharp for his own good, eh?'

But when DC looked again at where the traveller had been, she had already gone. Quite a surprise really, for him, as he was accustomed to doing the disappearing act himself.

He found her outside the courtroom, tears streaming down her face, watching a group of soldiers bent on a task. They were laughing and joking and roughly pushing each other in mock posturing, but one of them was making something on the ground, and it was to this soldier that Trav had gone. While the loud shouts of 'Crucify him, crucify him!' rang across the courtyard from the lips of the crowd, Trav stood staring down at the twisted circle of sticks and thorns being woven together in the soldier's hand.

'It's for him, isn't it?' she wept.

DC nodded, but could not speak.

'I almost chose this one,' she whispered through her tears. 'In my dream, DC, with the objects you gave me, I almost chose the crown of thorns, to change things, like you promised I could.'

'What would you have done with it, Trav?' he asked her.

'I would have offered to wear it for him, DC,' she replied.

'*You* wear it? Are you sure?'

'Well, no one can remove his dying agony. Even though Simon of Cyrene was able to carry the weight of the wood for a little way, only Jesus could grace the cross of Calvary. I know now that I could not, and should not, try to change that—and I could not ease any of his suffering.'

'I had to allow you to learn that lesson for yourself, Trav.'

'But I would have worn the crown with pride, for it would be a privilege, DC—every thorn-prick a royal duty and every drop of blood an honour.'

'You have spoken well,' said DC, smiling, 'and more accurately than you know. For you indeed bear all the heritage of a royal princess, daughter of the King of kings, and every painful duty of family relationship, work or poor health will adorn your forehead like crowning jewels. Wear it well, dear traveller, for each droplet from your forehead is precious blood, bought by his royal sacrifice, and one day you too shall walk free from an empty tomb in joy, to be with him for ever.'

Dear Lord, what do I do with your majesty? Could I choose a jewel for you to wear? Would the sound of my offerings of praise be a necklace for your forehead? Would a bracelet of my prayers adorn your wrist? Would my daily steps of obedience crown your head with glory? Or do my sins prick your skull with thorns of sadness? Do I stand with Pilate after all?

No, no, dear Lord, let me share your pain in every choice I make—embracing a thousand lesser daily crosses on my way through the labyrinth of this world's trials of head and heart and soul. Help me to bear each thorn with quiet determination, to cultivate the love that you have shown me and reflect it back to others. Help me to experience the truth that it is by embracing suffering, not with resignation but in your strength, that we find ourselves freed from the tyranny of pain in this world and the next. Amen

Saturday

JUST PASSING BY

They compelled a passer-by, who was coming in from the country, to carry his cross; it was Simon of Cyrene, the father of Alexander and Rufus. Then they brought Jesus to the place called Golgotha (which means the place of a skull). And they offered him wine mixed with myrrh; but he did not take it.

MARK 15:21–23

'But I say to you that listen, Love your enemies, do good to those who hate you, bless those who curse you, pray for those who abuse you. If anyone strikes you on the cheek, offer the other also; and from anyone who takes away your coat do not withhold even your shirt.'

LUKE 6:27–29

He was on his way up to Jerusalem, the man from Cyrene. Perhaps he was a Jew fulfilling his duty as a pilgrim at Passover, or on business, or maybe he was just passing through. Who knows why Simon of Cyrene happened to be in that particular place, at that specific moment? But what happened next changed his life and the life of his family for ever.

To the traveller it looked quite cruel, the way the soldiers roughly halted the passer-by, turning him in his tracks and forcing him to his knees. She bristled at the sight, her 21st-century assertiveness and acute concern about human rights rising to her throat. Why doesn't he protest, she fumed to herself, or even try to run away? What right have they to do this to an innocent bystander? But she had forgotten how Jesus, when speaking to the Jews about their enemies, had highlighted these very aspects of Roman treatment of the locals. A soldier was permitted to take whatever he needed from a native, on demand (Luke 6:27–29).

Simon had no redress, neither to Roman law, nor to future Western concepts of individual rights. He just happened, unfortunately, to be in the right place at the wrong time. Or was he? Trav wasn't watching the soldiers any more but gazing intently at the bent figure of Jesus as his body braced itself for the physical wrench as they roughly tore the crossbar off his shoulders and on to the ground. A pool of blood had already formed on the dirt in which he knelt, his wounds still dripping after the soldiers' treatment in the courtyard, the hair covering his forehead matted with the blood seeping from under the thorn-pricks of the crown.

It was the look in his eyes that she would never forget. Twisting his head to see what was happening to Simon, he gave the passer-by such a look of empathy and gratitude that Simon was no longer anticipating the weight of the wood or the welts from the ropes on his flesh as the soldiers carelessly transferred the crossbar from Jesus' body to his.

She envied Simon then. Of all the people whom God had placed in a position to help Jesus in his pain, only Simon had so far succeeded. Disciples, priests, lawyers, governors, dreamers, all had failed him, and this poor man, in from the country and just passing by, had succeeded where even she must fail. She longed to know more of this man. The Bible had told her so little. One thing was sure, though: if this was his first encounter with the living Christ, the story certainly did not end there. His two sons, Alexander and Rufus, had been well known to Mark when he came to write his Gospel. A whole family would one day be part of the victorious consequences of Christ's journey to Calvary, all because their father was in the right place at the wrong time. No—all because the Father God had placed Simon in exactly the right place at the right time; all because the creator knew the heart and mind of this quiet countryman and deemed him worthy to share in Christ's sufferings and not to let him down.

She longed to ask Simon questions: 'Were you around later, when Paul preached about sharing the suffering of Christ?' (Philippians 1:29; 3:10) or, 'Didn't you consider that one look of love from Jesus' face a thousand times more significant to your life than the hard struggle up the hill with that blood-soaked, heavy crossbar?' How could a man 'accidentally' help so well, she wondered, when so many, manipulative like Judas, or full of devotion like Peter, or pricked by conscience like Pilate, had failed miserably? Then she realized what Simon had done that the others had not. He had obeyed. Judas had disobeyed the command to submit his will to God's planning. Peter had forgotten that when he had obeyed Christ he could walk on water, so long as he did not take his eyes off Jesus to consider his own predicament. Pilate knew that the prisoner had done no wrong but could not obey his own conscience when it was prodded by God. Simon obeyed even his enemies, when the law compelled him to carry an alleged criminal's cross.

Dear Father, it is no coincidence that I stand where I stand today. I may be passing by, but please make me halt. Compel me by your love to look around and see what crosses I can carry in your name.

Look upon my suffering till I can see only the face of Jesus before my eyes—his tears for my wounds, his love for my fear, his smile of gratitude for my poor, small devotion. The hill is steep ahead, Lord. Let me climb it with you. Amen

THE FINAL FURLONG

Sunday

A KIND OF CORONATION

And they crucified him, and divided his garments among them, casting lots to decide what each should take. It was nine o'clock in the morning when they crucified him. The inscription of the charge against him read, 'The King of the Jews.'

MARK 15:24–26

Pilate also had an inscription written and put on the cross. It read, 'Jesus of Nazareth, the King of the Jews.' Many of the Jews read this inscription, for the place where Jesus was crucified was near the city; and it was written in Hebrew, in Latin, and in Greek. Then the chief priests of the Jews said to Pilate, 'Do not write, "The King of the Jews," but, "This man said, I am King of the Jews."' Pilate answered, 'What I have written I have written.'

JOHN 19:19–22

Just four words: 'And they crucified him.' That was all Mark could manage. Well, he wasn't there, was he? None of them was, none of the men except John. So Mark keeps it curt, clear and clinical. He tells of the soldiers casting lots for Christ's garments, he records the hour of the event, and he quotes the words of the inscription on the placard above the Lord's head. His record continues later with some details of what else was taking place round and about the central act upon the cross, but not a word do we hear from Jesus in Mark's account, until Christ's last breath on the cross. For an eye-witness account, only John's Gospel will do.

What would the traveller do at the top of that hill? Could she stand amid that baying, irreverent crowd and witness such scenes of utter barbarity inflicted upon her Master? The dream carrier got there before her and was anxiously searching the crowd. Many criminals had experienced this already and there would be more. He glanced with disgust at the small knot of soldiers already arguing over who should inherit the clothes of the dying. They would rip them to shreds if there was no other way to settle the dispute. Perks of the job, he thought with great sadness for the underpaid, overworked men who had to be the instruments of execution and then go home to their families or their own grim thoughts at the end of each gory day. They won't rip his robe, he thought, it is seamless, as the Boss had directed garments made for the holy priesthood to be (Exodus 28:32). Sure enough, they didn't, but instead cast lots for it, gambling over an item woven carefully and lovingly, perhaps by a woman who loved Jesus deeply.

In the crowd there were Romans, Jews, Greeks, all manner of nationalities, for Palestine was a crossroads of the known world at that time, thanks to the Roman roads and the steadily growing empire. Many were just passing through as Simon had been, but few stopped, as he had been given the honour to do. None was able to ease Christ's burden as the cross was raised high and dropped with a jarring thud into the hole dug for it in the ground. Everyone could read what the placard said above the alleged criminal's head, for it was written in Hebrew, Latin and Greek. Pilate had made his point in writing, sky high. His hands were washed, his finger was pointed at those who betrayed their own, and ironically, by the very inscription 'King of the Jews', his back-handed witness to the truth of the sovereignty of Jesus stood for all time, a memorial from the cross.

The dream carrier still could not find Trav. He pushed on between priests and workmen alike, between Pharisees and Sadducees, between court officials and common men. He saw Jesus refuse the wine and myrrh, the nearest thing available as an anaesthetic to deaden pain. DC paused momentarily to thank the Boss for taking the experience of the pain of the world's sin upon his shoulders without a clouded mind. But where was the traveller? Then he found her.

She did not look like a person at all—just a pile of clothing curled into a tight ball, huddled upon the ground at the forefront of the crowd, with her back to the cross and leaning her weight against three women who stood in devastating stillness, staring up at the figure hanging there and clinging to each other as if they were drowning. The dream carrier's foot caught the edge of the bundle and it brought him stumbling to his knees beside her.

'Trav,' he whispered with tears in his eyes, 'Trav, is that you?' She lifted her head towards the direction of his voice, but her eyes remained tightly shut and her body began to rock backwards and forwards in a desperate motion of self-comfort. 'I can't look,' she sobbed. 'Please don't ask me to look, DC.' He wanted to take her in his arms as a father would a child. He wanted to hold her so tightly that the nightmares would flee; he longed to wipe every tear from her eyes. Most of all, he longed to tell her the dream, the dream he had never carried, the one the Boss had dreamed himself. It was a dream of a perfect garden where no thorns grew and where all God's children could walk without fear; a dream of people made in the wonderful image of the creator—an incredible achievement—living in a universe teeming with life. It was the hope of a relationship between creator and creature which would bring fulfilment to the creature and great joy to both. He longed to tell her how, even though the first human couple had destroyed the beginnings of that dream by disobeying the Boss and making the world into a broken earth, the Father had never given up his dream or his creation, or his love for her, huddled as she was now at the foot of the cross.

'It's not over yet, Trav. The dream continues. This is part of the Boss's plan.'

'He's dying,' she sobbed.

'Yes, how else can justice be done? Someone has to pay the price for sin.'

'But it's not fair, DC, he is innocent.' Her tears would not stop. The dream carrier felt her pain deeply and wished he did not have to ask her his next question, but ask he must.

'Would you have us all pay, then, Trav?' His eyes were soft in the asking.

'It's too much,' she whispered. 'Nobody could pay for the world's sin unless...'

He was nodding now. 'Unless...?'

'Unless they were a God,' she almost choked out the answer.

'But he had to be human too, Trav, a human who lived and breathed and walked among humans; who struggled with temptation as you do, who endured the pain of the broken earth as you do, who wept as you do, yet without sinning. Only a God who walked in perfection upon the earth, as a man, could undo the harm done by Adam and Eve and pay the death sentence for us all.'

She hated her sin then, hated every tiny molecule of it. Suddenly that which once seemed so small to her was brought into clear focus by the instrument of the cross. Like a microscope, what was happening just a short distance from where she crouched brought magnification to the events and actions of her past life, and her sin seemed to take a form that was tangible in the stench of the blood and excrement discharged from the other prisoners undergoing execution. She saw sin for what it really was, a cancer to be slashed from her life as a surgeon wields his knife without compromise. Feeling naked upon the dirt ground, she felt the trembling bodies of the three women as she huddled closer against their backs. What could they see that she was too frightened to look upon? Was he looking down at them?

Dear Jesus, I wish I could blame Adam; I wish I could blame Eve, I wish I was at home in the 21st century with its rationalizations, its scientific arguments, its 'retail therapy' when we feel a little down. But I have smelt the stench of sin; I have cowered from loving eyes that wept upon a cross. I know better, because I have been afraid to watch you die. Forgive us when we hide from the cross. Amen

Monday

THE FAITHFUL ONES

Meanwhile, standing near the cross of Jesus were his mother, and his mother's sister, Mary the wife of Clopas, and Mary Magdalene. When Jesus saw his mother and the disciple whom he loved standing beside her, he said to his mother, 'Woman, here is your son.' Then he said to the disciple, 'Here is your mother.' And from that hour the disciple took her to his own home.

JOHN 19:25–27

Of all the disciples with their bluster and boasting of how they would go to their death for him, one only stood at the cross. Perhaps only a beloved disciple can be the kind of friend who sees the object of his love in pain and yet, with the strength of their shared love, does not run away. John's suffering is not recorded; his eyes were on Jesus.

Like a loved one nursing a terminally ill relative to their death, he must have felt every shudder, every sob, every facial spasm of agony as though he was experiencing it himself. As those who sit by the hospital beds of beloved ones know, it is often harder to watch a loved one suffer than to go through the horror yourself. But John, who had fled with the others from Gethsemane, did not fail Jesus at the cross. It was this proven faithfulness that gained for John the greatest honour of all, the trust of his Master.

'Listen!' said the dream carrier to a distraught Trav, as the general chatter and hubbub of the scene was interrupted by a sound coming from one of the crosses. At first it was difficult to hear the voice of Jesus above the noise of the crowd, but then, as he called again to the little knot of women standing below, watcher after watcher shushed and nudged each other into silence to eavesdrop on his conversation.

'Woman,' he said, and although there were many around it was Mary who raised her eyes to meet the gaze of her dying son, 'here is your son!' Trav did not look around but kept her head lowered, her eyes closed, but she imagined John stepping forward towards Mary and taking her in his arms as Jesus' words rang out, 'Here is your mother!' In the midst of his pain and agony, when the entire weight of the world's sin was about to make itself felt upon his shoulders, when he was about to experience the devastation of a momentary barrier of sin separating him from the Father, at this time Jesus first secured a home and a future for his mother, and a mother for his beloved disciple. They would both need each other dearly in the months and years to come.

Was this the moment when Trav felt the weight slip from her heart—when she realized without a shadow of a doubt that this same Jesus who was faithful to his loved ones and disciples, even from a cross, would be faithful to her? DC could not say exactly how or when it happened but slowly, very slowly, he saw Trav uncurl her taut limbs, raise her head, and with hesitation rise to her feet. He reached out his hand to steady her progress but she had turned around and was looking closely, not upwards, but into the faces of Mary the mother of Jesus, and Mary his aunt, and Mary Magdalene his devoted friend. Suddenly she was part of their group, their love and agony mixed also within her soul. She desperately wanted him to stay, yet she knew that if he did not die, hope would never find a home again in humankind.

For that hope to blossom, this Mary who had borne him would have to stand and watch her son die. What sharper sword could there be than this? (Luke 2:35). For hope to grow, this Mary who had helped to support the family as his aunt would walk through long avenues of grief and mourning with her sister, to help her find the light of a new day. For hope to find a home, she whom they called Mary of Magdala would have to journey to a dark tomb of despair and, with eyes of faith, believe the unbelievable until she clearly heard him call her name and could know, without a doubt, that it was for this that he had come.

The traveller shuddered and pulled her coat more tightly around her body. She had not yet looked upwards—her eyes still avoided the cross—but her mind was full of wonderings. What might the Master still ask her to do before her life was finished? Would she be able to emulate these three faithful women and John to the very end? Could it be that, even now, she had failed him on her journey to Calvary, unable to look upon his blood-stained face?

DC watched her move slowly away from the cross, walking as though in a stupor. Believing her to be in shock, he followed her through the crowd, calling softly and insistently. 'Trav,' he called, 'it's not over yet. You must not go; there is so much to tell.'

'Tell me then, DC,' she answered wearily. 'Tell me what I've missed.'

Dear Lord, one day I'll walk with you without the stain of sin and on that day I'll let your pain gain entrance to my soul. For on that day death will be fully dead and pain can no longer hold me hostage. When faith becomes my friend, no longer duty, I'll know it was the product of your love, and if our eyes would touch across the centuries I'll know it was not the turning of my head that grazed my heart and set my hope alive but rather the soft and steady gaze of how you looked on me from the torturous miracle of the cross. Amen

Tuesday

ON SIMILAR CROSSES

Two others also, who were criminals, were led away to be put to death with him. When they came to the place that is called The Skull, they crucified Jesus there with the criminals, one on his right and one on his left. Then Jesus said, 'Father, forgive them; for they do not know what they are doing.' ...

One of the criminals who were hanged there kept deriding him and saying, 'Are you not the Messiah? Save yourself and us!' But the other rebuked him, saying, 'Do you not fear God, since you are under the same sentence of condemnation? And we indeed have been condemned justly; for we are getting what we deserve for our deeds, but this man has done nothing wrong.' Then he said, 'Jesus, remember me when you come into your kingdom.' He replied, 'Truly I tell you, today you will be with me in Paradise.'

LUKE 23:32–34, 39–43

The dream carrier began to describe to the traveller what she had not seen. He told her of other crosses that had given her no pain because her thoughts had been on the unfolding drama of the central cross.

'I don't need to know this, DC,' she protested in frustration. 'Can't you see? It's hard enough for me to face the dying of Jesus without worrying about real criminals who deserve everything that's coming to them.' The moment she said it, she felt guilty; it sounded insensitive. 'I'm sorry. Go on, then, tell me about the others.'

His description did not need to be too graphic. She had already seen the crosses erected and was aware of others standing on either side of the Master's cross, but had taken no notice of the two criminals who flanked the central action.

'This one,' said DC, miming to his right, 'took out all his frustrations on Jesus and blamed the Lord fully for the predicament that the other criminals found themselves in. "Save yourself and us!" he yelled, as if he had a right to salvation on demand. Know anybody like that, Trav?'

She blushed at the thought of rather too many occupants of her home church pews who, Sunday after Sunday, expected 'salvation on demand' without giving a thought to the possibility that their rightful place might well be upon a criminal's cross. Might she ever have been one of them?

'It is so difficult in my time, DC,' she explained. 'The very word "sin" has gone out of fashion. When people's consciences are pricked by seeing immoral actions all around them, they dare not protest for fear of being accused of making "value judgments", and when they feel guilty about something they have done contrary to God's commands in the Bible, well, there are plenty of voices to insist that they shouldn't worry because "everyone is doing it". Each person's opinion is elevated to the extent that absolutes are disintegrating, and where art once reflected life, now life often apes the behaviour of the current most popular soap opera characters.'

DC was listening quietly to the tirade of genuine frustration, and when she paused to draw breath, he quietly asked, 'So you don't feel able to choose a cross, then?'

She blinked. What on earth was he talking about? He mimed to his left and continued, 'On the other side of Jesus, another criminal was paying his rightful dues on a similar cross.'

'What had he done?' she queried.

'As a matter of fact, I'm not sure,' said DC. 'But it really doesn't matter.'

'It doesn't?'

'No. Sin is just sin, Trav, everything from a so-called white lie to full-scale murder, it's all disobedience to God's loving commands and every part of it grieves his spirit.'

'You want me to choose between these two crosses, and you say they are equally guilty. Well, then, what is there to choose between?'

DC smiled patiently. 'The second man wasn't shifting blame. He knew what he had done and was ashamed of it. He acknowledged his guilt and appeared to know of Christ's innocence and something more. When he asked the Lord, "Remember me when you come into your kingdom", he showed great faith—faith that there was more to life than planet Earth and that Christ had the power and authority that he had claimed to have, power over life and death and eternity.

'It was real repentance, Trav, and you know what? Jesus said, "Yes." He actually promised that criminal a place in his eternal kingdom right there and then, while they hung on those crosses.'

She didn't have to answer DC then. She knew that he knew that there was no contest. Who would choose the cross of the damned when forgiveness was offered, full and free, in response to Jesus? She wished she could fly home right then, for thousands, perhaps millions, inside the Church and beyond its doors were nailed right now to the wrong crosses and did not know, or had forgotten, the necessity for making a choice before it was too late.

'You can tell them later, Trav,' said DC, reading her thoughts, 'but first you have to decide whether to return to Calvary or keep running away.'

She knew that she must turn around and retrace her steps. Christ was still on the cross and she must look into his face. The thought terrified her. What would she see there? It is true that he had said, 'Father, forgive them; for they do not know what they are doing', and if he forgave his enemies and the criminal who had repented, she need have no fear. But what agony would she see written there, what pain, what fear as he hung on the cross? To know that her sin through the years was still contributing to such sorrow... she could not bear it. But she had to go.

As she, and DC with her, stepped forward to return to the cross, the dream carrier held out his arm to halt her in her steps. 'It is finished,' he whispered as though he had heard Jesus speak those very words. 'Look!' and the dream carrier pointed to the sky.

It was getting dark, very dark, despite its being only the sixth hour. For three hours, until the ninth hour, she could not see her way ahead to walk even one single step.

Dear Lord, forgive every moment I waste or delay in telling others of your saving offer of life. You warn us, again and again, to 'work the works of him who sent me while it is day; night is coming when no one can work' (John 9:4).

Will I never see your face because of the darkness all around? Shine your light, the light of your truth down the centuries to illuminate our steps, in church, in shopping malls, in schools and hospitals, banks and leisure centres. Shine your light through me, and may not a moment be lost in helping weary travellers to find their way to Calvary and beyond. Amen

Wednesday

GOD'S HIDDEN FACE

From noon on, darkness came over the whole land until three in the afternoon. And about three o'clock Jesus cried with a loud voice, 'Eli, Eli, lema sabachthani?' that is, 'My God, my God, why have you forsaken me?' When some of the bystanders heard it, they said, 'This man is calling for Elijah.' At once one of them ran and got a sponge, filled it with sour wine, put it on a stick, and gave it to him to drink. But the others said, 'Wait, let us see whether Elijah will come to save him.' Then Jesus cried again with a loud voice and breathed his last. At that moment the curtain of the temple was torn in two, from top to bottom. The earth shook, and the rocks were split. The tombs also were opened, and many bodies of the saints who had fallen asleep were raised. After his resurrection they came out of the tombs and entered the holy city and appeared to many.

MATTHEW 27:45–53

She had seen horror movies before. They were not her favourite form of recreation, but at least they weren't real. This was real!

The cry of the dying Christ reached her ears in the darkness, a cry of such pain and devastation, of such desolation, that she thought her heart would break with it. She knew for all time, with the surety of shared pain, that Jesus was taking upon himself at that moment the loneliness of humanity separated from the creator. For that brief moment in time, he experienced the full weight of the broken earth's sin and the obliteration of his Father's face from view, for God cannot look upon sin.

For that brief span of time, too, the traveller realized something of what hell must be like. Even in earth's worst moments, God is not absent from the globe. Even when pestilence and famine, violence and evil stalk the earth, the presence of God is still freely available to all who call to him. But in that moment, Jesus felt what it was like for God to turn his face and look away, what it was like to be truly alone.

No wonder the bystanders believed that the end of the world had come. Was he calling Elijah, they wondered—a forerunner to the Messiah, one who, by tradition, would appear again at the end? There was darkness, pain, the terror of the confused crowd that must have scattered blindly in all directions when the sun's light failed. There were howls of outrage and fear as the Holy of Holies, the most sacred and hidden part of the temple where only priests could go, was dramatically exposed for all to see when the curtain dividing it from the people suddenly ripped from top to bottom.

The traveller could not see it all, but the earth beneath her feet shook until the very rocks split open. She had never experienced an earthquake before and was terrified. In that arid land, the ground cracked like sandpaper, and cliffs and craggy hilltops came tumbling down, flattening everything in their path. Around Jerusalem every available cave had been claimed as a fitting tomb for the dead, and now, with rockfalls and earthquake, the contents of those caves were laid open. Howls of fear and amazement assaulted Trav's ears as person after person pushed and shoved her in the darkness, running in terror from the tombs, calling out warnings about the dead whom they had seen emerge from those tombs and head towards the city. And all the while, the dying criminals on their separate crosses relinquished their life-blood to the earth.

If ever she might have wished she had not come, it was now. She was running too, hard and fast and without thought. Unheeding of the ground opening up before her, uncaring of who stood in her way, blind panic at its very worst seized her, and the heaving mass of the crowd around carried all before them. Suddenly strong arms closed around her and held her fast. She struggled but could not break free, trapped in the darkness.

'Stop!' DC insisted, his voice commanding, his vice-like grip tightening around her shoulders. 'Stop, you're going the wrong way.'

She felt a mixture of relief and terror at his actions. 'I can't go back, DC!' she screamed. 'Don't make me!'

He released his grasp but she could still feel his breath upon her hair, and his nearness calmed her enough for her to hear what he was saying.

'You must return to the cross,' he said.

'But he's dying.'

'Yes, you must return and hear his prayer.'

'I heard him pray, DC. It was awful.' She was shaking from head to foot now as the shock began to wear off. 'He is forsaken, desolate,' she sobbed, 'I cannot bear it.'

'But he is still praying, Trav, he has not stopped praying. You must hear his final prayer. Please come.'

How she got there, she could not tell—perhaps DC carried her, maybe she stumbled back—but it seemed only an instant later that she looked upwards into the darkness and saw only the brooding shape of the cross, an empty shadow against a lightening sky. It was still too dark to see his face. But his voice, his voice was a mere dove's wing away as with calm and resolute clarity she heard him say, 'Father, into your hands I commend my spirit' (Luke 23:46).

A cry of joy escaped from DC's lips as he sank to the ground, tears flowing from his face, his strong arms raised to the cross in worship. 'His mother taught him that prayer, Trav,' he whispered, 'and Joseph too. It is a child's prayer. Each night, before sleep, every Jewish child says such a thing. Don't you see, Trav? He is not destroyed, he is trusting his Father, he is resting in the love that he knows will never fail him—yes, trusting even now.'

Dear God, make me a child again, to sleep without fear, to walk alone and know you will never leave me, to trust the one who walked the path of earth's terror and won the battle for us all—the one who trusted you and knew no disappointment in the end. Amen

Thursday

EYE WITNESS

Since it was the day of Preparation, the Jews did not want the bodies left on the cross during the sabbath, especially because that sabbath was a day of great solemnity. So they asked Pilate to have the legs of the crucified men broken and the bodies removed. Then the soldiers came and broke the legs of the first and of the other who had been crucified with him. But when they came to Jesus and saw that he was already dead, they did not break his legs. Instead, one of the soldiers pierced his side with a spear, and at once blood and water came out. (He who saw this has testified so that you also may believe. His testimony is true, and he knows that he tells the truth.) These things occurred so that the scripture might be fulfilled, 'None of his bones shall be broken.' And again another passage of scripture says, 'They shall look on the one whom they have pierced.'

JOHN 19:31–37

The traveller never fully considered herself an eye witness. A time-traveller only 'visits', but John was there. On that fateful day before the sabbath, when all hell seemed to loose itself in earthquake and darkness upon the unsuspecting population of Jerusalem, John remained by the cross.

As light returned to the chaotic scene and the officials and soldiers, under orders from the authority, attempted to regain a sense of control, their immediate problem was how to effect a clean and speedy clear-up job. Since the following day, Saturday, was the Sabbath and a special festival Sabbath at that, the remains of criminals and suchlike must be well away by dusk, so the clear-up job had to be done without delay. At all costs, religious niceties must be observed and the Sabbath kept holy and without blemish, so the Jews asked Pilate to have the criminals' legs broken. This was often done to add to the punishment but, in this case, it was to hasten death and aid effective disposal of the remains.

For John, it proved to be yet another confirmation of prophecy fulfilled, for, having broken the legs of the other occupants of the crosses, they found Jesus already dead and did not do the same to him. John must have thanked the Father for sparing his Master the protracted death that the criminals suffered. To John, Jesus was indeed the perfect replacement sacrifice for the Passover lamb (Exodus 12:46; Numbers 9:12). How this beloved disciple agonized over his friend's suffering, noticing every development in the horrific saga, imbuing the spear-thrust to Christ's side with more meaning from scripture (Zechariah 12:10). Perhaps it is only those who fully appreciate the cost of the sacrifice that Jesus made and, in love, know his pain, who can then grasp the significance of the creator's unremitting dream from the beginning of time to the cross and beyond. John, the beloved disciple, whose head had rested upon the Lord's breast at the last supper, knew.

Another eye witness who was there that day also knew the truth, not because he had lain close enough to the Master's breast to feel his pain, but because he stood facing that pain as Jesus breathed his last. The centurion, just doing his job, nevertheless kept his eyes, ears and mind fully open to observe the facts. He heard Jesus forgive his enemies, and who better than the chief soldier on guard to know what Jesus had been through at the hands of his enemies? He saw him show compassion to the women, to John, and to the repentant criminal, and who better than the head soldier to know of what Jesus had been falsely accused in the kangaroo courts? Who better than the centurion to know, at first hand, how the Lord had behaved during his degrading treatment from soldiers and crowd alike; and now, at the last, who better than he to watch Jesus die and to be qualified to compare his death with who knows how many others that month, that year, that full period of Roman occupation? This Roman, this professional officer, this man of authority of the ruling establishment was there to testify to what most of the disciples, in their absence, could not: 'Truly this man was God's Son!' (Mark 15:39).

Dear Jesus, open our minds to see what the world tries to mask. Break down the walls of doubt and scepticism and fear until we stand, unafraid, before your cross and see you as you truly are, the saviour of our lives— you the perfect sacrifice and we the sinners. Then can we lay our heads upon your breast in full submission and take forgiveness like a dying thief. Amen

Good Friday

HIDDEN VICTORY

A great number of the people followed him, and among them were women who were beating their breasts and wailing for him. But Jesus turned to them and said, 'Daughters of Jerusalem, do not weep for me, but weep for yourselves and for your children. For the days are surely coming when they will say, "Blessed are the barren, and the wombs that never bore, and the breasts that never nursed." Then they will begin to say to the mountains, "Fall on us"; and to the hills, "Cover us." For if they do this when the wood is green, what will happen when it is dry?'
LUKE 23:27–31

They called it good, this travesty of justice,
This devastating form of human pride,
That brought an innocent to spill his lifeblood,
Where Eden's thorns entrapped, and scourged, and lied,
And he the very one who warned them of it
As women wailed and trudged for pity's sake.
And who would stand today and tell the tale
Where terror bombs and innocents still wail?

Would Palestine dispose of ageless weapons?
Would Belfast offer up my rights for his?
Would olive tree and olive branch entwine together
to bleed,

to pray,
to fall asleep in swathes of history,
to waken within sound of mystery
As mystery weeps and bleeds and kneels within Gethsemane?

And as we live our petty lives and brief,
Is there time still to walk those dusty streets,
And look upon the love of God made man?
Till in the true submission of our lives
We break the sword, and heal the ear,
And ride instead the donkey to the feast.
For if the answer's 'no'
Can we ever claim the right to name the day
And call this Friday good?

For prayer: keep silence at the cross. Let Jesus speak.

Saturday

LOVE BY STEALTH

After these things, Joseph of Arimathea, who was a disciple of Jesus, though a secret one because of his fear of the Jews, asked Pilate to let him take away the body of Jesus. Pilate gave him permission; so he came and removed his body. Nicodemus, who had at first come to Jesus by night, also came, bringing a mixture of myrrh and aloes, weighing about a hundred pounds. They took the body of Jesus and wrapped it with the spices in linen cloths, according to the burial custom of the Jews. Now there was a garden in the place where he was crucified, and in the garden there was a new tomb in which no one had ever been laid. And so, because it was the Jewish day of Preparation, and the tomb was nearby, they laid Jesus there.

JOHN 19:38–42

The next day, that is, after the day of Preparation, the chief priests and the Pharisees gathered before Pilate and said, 'Sir, we remember what that impostor said while he was still alive, "After three days I will rise again." Therefore command the tomb to be made secure until the third day; otherwise his disciples may go and steal him away, and tell the people, "He has been raised from the dead," and the last deception would be worse than the first.' Pilate said to them, 'You have a guard of soldiers; go, make it as secure as you can.' So they went with the guard and made the tomb secure by sealing the stone.

MATTHEW 27:62–66

Joseph of Arimathea, the well-respected member of the Council, the one who was genuinely seeking the kingdom of God (Mark 15:43), found real courage that day. He stepped out from under the cloak of secrecy and risked everything—his job, his respect within society, his salary, his family's security and, as he stood before Pilate, perhaps even his life.

The traveller watched as Joseph was admitted into the governor's presence. With great style he was issued in, with a flourish, almost a fanfare, of which he was worthy as a high member of the Council. The shocked look upon Pilate's face when Joseph requested permission to take the body for burial said it all. The traveller could not believe it when Pilate signed the papers to release the body into Joseph's hands. What was the governor thinking? she wondered. Did he fully comprehend that Joseph was a secret disciple? Why else would he care what happened to the body? Did Pilate, by that stage, just want rid of the whole affair, trusting Joseph enough not to embarrass the Council or himself any further? Or did his conscience still bother him enough to prompt him to grasp at this last straw of appeasement towards all that Jesus stood for, believing that the least he could do was to treat the dead body with respect? She could not tell, Pilate was well trained in hiding his feelings. But he took time to ensure that the prisoner was fully dead before releasing the body into Joseph's care (Mark 15:44).

One other person came with Joseph to remove the body. Watching the care with which Nicodemus brought the mixture of myrrh and aloes weighing a hundred pounds—an expensive burden to carry—the traveller was reminded of the scene, some days before, when Mary had anointed Jesus' feet and wiped them dry with her hair. No longer under cover of darkness, Nicodemus was also openly risking everything to identify with the Lord. Had his long conversation with Jesus borne fruit (John 3:1–12)? Had Nicodemus recognized what Christ had done for him on the cross? Did the Lord's dying bring this secret seeker of truth to understand that he must die to all but Christ in order to be truly born again? He had already tried to show love by stealth, by defending Jesus up to a point (John 7:50).

Now both Nicodemus and Joseph exposed their devotion to the light of day and took upon themselves the menial task of binding the body in preparation for burial. Laying the dead Christ, with such lavish commitment, in a brand new tomb in a garden, they gave to one who, in life, had walked the paths of the poorest of the poor a rich man's funeral in Joseph's tomb. The love by stealth of both men had been called to light, and now their actions gave testimony of their devotion to the Master.

She wondered whether Joseph's vote had been the only one to disagree with the Council's decision to kill Jesus (Luke 23:50). She wondered how many in her century betrayed Christ daily by their silence, or their surrender to peer pressure, or fear of embarrassment, or worry about what they might lose if the truth came out. She wondered how many times her actions, or lack of them, had nailed him to the cross.

It was with reverence and care that Joseph and Nicodemus had supervised the rolling of the huge boulder to close the entrance of the cave-tomb while Mary Magdalene and Mary, Christ's aunt, watched. The women sat opposite the cave, their vigil complete from cross to tomb. Soon they must return home to minister to a widow and bereaved mother whose grief was beyond speech. They could tell her then, tell her of the loving care her son had finally received in death. How that mother must have thanked the two men who had 'loved by stealth' and now had garnered, through Christ's death, the strength from God to love beyond the point of fear.

Dear Lord, give such strength to all who sit opposite tombs this night. May those who weep tears of grief, and who lie without hope in the waiting hours, know that you have gone before to bring a new dawn, yes, even to broken hearts.

Whatever seals the tomb of their joy, as Pilate sealed your tomb, may they discover in your time that you have come to break the seal and set them free.

Please, Lord, confuse the soldiers who stand guard to hold hostage peace of mind, who awaken those who try to sleep with thoughts of bitterness of yesterday or terror for tomorrow. May they be overcome, as soldiers can be, by the gentle power of the Spirit's healing touch, and may each grief-stained heart both find and give forgiveness for all the hurts that waylaid their steps and took them far from Calvary.

Tonight it is dark, Lord, and soldiers guard the entrance to the place where you lie. But Jesus, it cannot stay like this, for you have dreamed a dream at the Father's side from the dawn of time—and you saw me within that dream. Thank you, thank you, God. Amen

Easter Sunday

ARISE!

But Mary stood weeping outside the tomb. As she wept, she bent over to look into the tomb; and she saw two angels in white, sitting where the body of Jesus had been lying, one at the head and the other at the feet. They said to her, 'Woman, why are you weeping?' She said to them, 'They have taken away my Lord, and I do not know where they have laid him.' When she had said this, she turned around and saw Jesus standing there, but she did not know that it was Jesus. Jesus said to her, 'Woman, why are you weeping? Whom are you looking for?' Supposing him to be the gardener, she said to him, 'Sir, if you have carried him away, tell me where you have laid him, and I will take him away.' Jesus said to her, 'Mary!' She turned and said to him in Hebrew, 'Rabboni!' (which means Teacher). Jesus said to her, 'Do not hold on to me, because I have not yet ascended to the Father. But go to my brothers and say to them, "I am ascending to my Father and your Father, to my God and your God."' Mary Magdalene went and announced to the disciples, 'I have seen the Lord'; and she told them that he had said these things to her.

JOHN 20:11–18 (READ ALSO MARK 16:1–20)

It was dawn, the first pale fingers of the sun's rising light spreading pointers of shadow across the garden, sketching the silhouette of trees upon the ground. Once more the dream carrier was searching. He had searched all night for the traveller but could not find her. Now, on the first day of a new week, he could not believe she was gone. Not today, he thought, you cannot give up today, Trav. You must come here today, and witness this new dawn. But the garden was empty and terribly still; no dawn chorus yet disturbed the air.

It was the soft footfalls of the women that he heard first. They came with an urgency to tend the body of Jesus as was the custom, treading carefully so as not to trample Joseph's lovely garden, and speaking only fleetingly in reverent whispers, as though already in the presence of greatness. He smiled at them as they passed, although they could not see him —the Lord's caring aunt, faithfully discharging her duty for her sister; Salome, whose prayer and financial support had upheld much of the Lord's ministry while he toured on the road from town to town; and Mary of Magdala, ever at his side, faithful even to the cross—but no Trav.

The three women had reached the tomb now and DC thrilled with joy to hear their cries as they found it empty. He waited at a distance to allow the messenger, stationed in angelic splendour past the point where soldiers once had stood, to tell them the good news that Christ had risen from the dead. But they were afraid and ran for their lives—all except Mary Magdalene. He wished he could shout to them then. He wanted to cry out what the angel had said: 'He is not here. Go, tell the others!' But it was not his task to do so. Instead he walked sadly in Mary's footsteps as she sobbed in confusion, shock and grief—and still there was no sign of the traveller.

Slowly, every particle of his being began to reverberate with echoes of glorious sound and light, and the pulse of a million galaxies began to fill him, like water pouring from a reservoir when the sluice gates open and the life-giving flood is restricted no more. He stopped quickly. He knew he must go no further because Mary and he were no longer alone in the garden. The Master, he realized, was very close at hand and, as a candle's light dissolves in bright sunlight, DC knew he could not eavesdrop upon their wonderful conversation. The Lord was calling Mary's name and turning her tears to joy.

The dream carrier was almost distraught now. He had searched everywhere, and the traveller who had gone through so much to walk to Calvary in the Master's footsteps could still not be found. 'Trav!' he called, resting momentarily against the outer walls of the tomb. 'Trav, I don't know where else to look. Where are you?' It was her tears that led him to her. He saw them, tiny droplets of wetness at the entrance to the tomb, leading a trail in the dusty sandstone right inside to where she was curled tight, knees to chin, sobbing muffled cries, arms wrapped around her head. She was curled upon the other grave-slab, the space reserved for future burials, forming a T-shape with the empty slab where Christ once lay. DC looked upon the Master's empty grave, the ceremonial bindings of death scattered where Peter had dropped them in shock and joy as he ran to tell the others that it was true—what Mary had tried to tell them was true. Jesus was alive!

The dream carrier reached gentle arms to hold her then, this time-traveller from another century who had carried so much pain to Calvary and watched her Master die without ever looking deep into his face. Now she'd missed him—or thought she had. Missed the glorious moment when the broken earth shuddered its last claims, death's claim of masterdom, and bowed at last to the supremacy of him who conquers all, Lord Jesus Christ.

'The dream now lives,' DC whispered in her ear, 'the one that always was too big for me to carry, the one the Father and the Son dreamt with the Spirit before the earth was new. Would you stay here in the tomb when, two thousand years from now, your touch is badly needed, to reach an era where many long to hear the healing news of Calvary? Such will be your joy. Come from the tomb! He calls you. Shake off whatever binds you here, for Mary dances even as we speak, and disciples watch him walk through walls—those same poor souls who once were racked with fear.'

Dear Lord, was it you who made this new season issue forth from winter's sleep? The day I started on my journey, buried spring had not yet broken through the darkness of the earth. But all around, the days are lengthening and light has come.

How dare I slumber on while this generation dies a little more each day for lack of you. You led me safe through desert pain and Calvary's horror, in the footsteps of the one who knew the victory to come.

Open up my eyes to see, not yesterday, but bright tomorrow, and in your promises of resurrection lead me home. Amen

AFTERWORD

He has a dream for you, dear traveller, whether you return to your own day in teens or twenties, or whether grey hairs already claim their place. It makes no difference, for you have been to Calvary and can never more stand ignorant of the truth. Now the choice is yours. What will you do with Jesus, when all around, your world bays for blood? You cannot wash the blood from Pilate's hands, or untie the noose from Judas as he hangs; nor can you stop the cockerel's crow in Peter's heart. But if you are brave enough to be a child again, it's not too late to seek the face of Jesus where you stand.

Go home, dear traveller, for he waits there for you—a risen saviour holding out forgiveness, love and joy—but you will never rise with him until you die the death to self and pride and sin. Then, walking through from tomb to world, broken as it is, you'll feel his hand upon your life and know that it was his idea that you should come, and walk for ever in his footsteps till he safely leads you home.

PRAYER OF COMMITMENT

The following prayer is for anyone who, through group study or by personal reading of this book, has heard the challenge, 'What will you do with Jesus?' and who wishes fervently to make a decision to accept him as their Master and Lord. It is a simple framework prayer for all ages, to be used by those who wish to make full commitment to him for salvation.

Jesus, I come to you now. I know you are here and you love me. I know that you gave your life for me on the cross. I believe you are God's Son, and I have faith that what you did at Calvary made it possible for me to receive forgiveness for my sins. I am sorry for all that I have done wrong. Please forgive me and help me to turn from wrongdoing. Please begin a new relationship with me now. I accept you into my life, not just as a friend or teacher, but as Master and Saviour. I open the door to the will of God the Father, I engage as a disciple of Jesus the Saviour and Lord, and I accept the guidance and indwelling of the Holy Spirit in all that I do from here on. Amen

You have completed the journey to Calvary. May your church, your minister, your fellowship, your group, support, nurture, teach, love and encourage you from here on, for the journey continues for a lifetime. Whatever happens, remember, Jesus said, 'I am with you always, to the end of the age' (Matthew 28:20). Trust him!

DISCUSSION STARTERS FOR SEVEN WEEKLY SESSIONS

Coming together as a group to accomplish any task always presents its own initial ice-breaking challenge, no matter how well the individuals know one another at the start. It might be encouraging, therefore, for each group member to bring to the first meeting an item or story, or both, which represents the experience of a past Lenten journey that they have made. For example, they might bring a set of weighing scales to represent the 'diet' that didn't work, or a pair of trainers that established the long-standing habit of a healthy lifestyle, or a short excerpt from a previous Lent book which particularly spoke to an individual and helped them to maintain momentum on their pilgrimage. Sharing together in smaller groups of five or seven (or, if they already know each other well, in pairs), the humour and/or profundity of the items or stories will not only establish rapport and motivate group commitment for the forthcoming weeks, but it can also be instrumental in identifying both helpful and mistaken concepts involved in the Lenten journey.

ASH WEDNESDAY TO SATURDAY: THE BATTLE

- With which of the traveller's pre-travel reservations can you identify? Are there any other reservations that a 21st-century pilgrim might experience?

- The wilderness was literal in the Palestine of two thousand years ago. For us in today's world, what kind of 'wilderness' threatens to dampen our spirits or slow our progress towards God? (Identify aspects of environment, lifestyle, habits, institutions and so on which contribute to the wilderness experience.) What deep needs does our own personal 'wilderness' engender in us, and how can we partner a loving God to begin to have those needs met and to help meet the needs of others?

- Have we considered the dark role that Satan plays in our lives? If not, why not? From ignorance? From concern about losing the balance between fear of Satan and confidence in the greater strength of Christ? (1 John 4:4). Or do we have the commendable desire not to deny responsibility for our acts or decisions or to blame others for our weaknesses? How can we achieve the right Christian balance in our understanding of this dark force at work in the world?

- Have we underestimated the power of the word of God to help us in our spiritual struggles? How well do we know it? How much do we consult it?

- Consider each of the three temptations that Satan used to tempt Christ in the desert. Do you recognize any 'echoes' of these in your own life?

WEEK ONE: THE ARMOUR

- Highlight each piece of spiritual armour from Ephesians 6 in turn and explore ways it might be wielded in this century to combat today's attacks of the 'Bad 'Un'.

- If your group is a youth group (or adults with a good sense of humour), it can be helpful to acquire some 'armour' props, such as motorbike helmet, plastic sword and so on. Try your local party costume and hats shop, or ask folk to search their attics, or get out the cardboard and sticky tape and have a creative armour-making workshop. (A mock 'battle' at the end might be fun and memorable for those who enjoy drama.) This kind of workshop certainly cements group interaction at the outset of the pilgrimage and ensures effective reinforcement of the pointers discussed.

WEEK TWO: THE DREAMERS

- Consider Jesus as the 'suffering servant'. How does sharing in his sufferings (Philippians 3:10; 1 Peter 4:13) fit into our dreams, ambitions, desires for our future? How does this concept revolutionize our pains and aches, failures and weaknesses, and strengthen our resolve to have mastery over them in the daily struggles of life? Whose suffering did we relieve a little this week? How much suffering or distress did we cause this week?

- Does the modern world conspire to 'dilute' the concept of sin? How much of a 'sinner' dare we admit to being? Have we truly repented? Have we experienced how much he truly loves us? Is 'holiness' becoming a 'non-word' today? Even as Christians, do we feel we need to apologize for desiring it? How can we understand the concept better without becoming conceited?

- What's my 'baby'? To what or whom are you clinging so tightly that you cannot dedicate it to God? Either identify it privately in silent prayer or share with the group for prayer.

- Discuss the universal roots of fear—past failure, vulnerability, childhood experiences, Satan's undermining of our confidence, lack of trust in God. Identify people around the world facing a 'lions' den' today and pray for them. Are there any more subtle threats of persecution within our own situations? Discuss ways by which our personal faith and trust can be strengthened—Bible study, prayer, fellowship, counselling, mentoring, worship, facing the feared threat in Christ's strength. Discuss relevant local challenges and obstacles to witnessing for Jesus and how they might be overcome. Perhaps share stories of past experiences of answered prayer from God in personal 'lions' den' situations.

- Despite knowing better, do we sometimes feel that God is far 'up there' and hard to reach? How close to us and our concerns can we bear to allow God to come, and do we believe in a fresh start? If possible, take time to have group prayer for any who have indicated that they wish to 'start again'.

- Identify the areas of enslavement in modern society. The group might take time to intercede in prayer for those in bondage to one or other of the shackles identified. What pursuits or lifestyles or ambitions diminish our growth in spirit?

- How much do we expect God to surprise us? Would we be prepared to do surprising things in unexpected places for him? Have we experienced a true sense of belonging to Christ? (Romans 8:14–17; Philippians 3:20).

- What part does God play in the hopes and dreams that we allow ourselves to have on earth? (Philippians 2:13; Jeremiah 29:11).

- When thinking of heaven, can we look forward with great expectation and, at the same time, embrace earth to the full while we are here? (John 10:10; 14:1–3; 17:15).

WEEK THREE: CALLED AND EQUIPPED

- In terms of following Jesus, it might be beneficial to look at two further passages: Matthew 5:1–14 and Matthew 10:16–20, 24–33. Peter, Judas and indeed all of the disciples disappointed Jesus at some point during Holy Week, despite many protestations of good intentions beforehand. How far would we be prepared to go to 'follow him'? Are we still selecting how much control he has over our lives, or is he Master in every sense? Have we explored the possibilities of using all our talents for him? Do we doubt what he can do with the smallest offering from our storehouse of qualifications, gifts, skills or hobbies?

- Prayer and action: are they well 'married' in our lives? The group might draw up a list of daily 'needs must' activities—eat, sleep, take the children to school and so on—and estimate how much time is allocated to each per week. Then take 'duty bound' commitments—visiting an elderly relative or friend, for example. Then consider quality 'switch off' time—on the golf course, in front of the TV or behind a book.

In which category would you place prayer time? At what point in our lives will we make Jesus' priorities our own?

- How do we cope with failure? Discuss past ineffective strategies for coping and hear each other's suggestions. Discuss other ways in which group members have succeeded in training themselves to focus upon Christ at times of failure and disappointment. Ask what God wants us to learn from this.

- Discuss the experience of loss (with sensitivity). Give time for feelings about bereavement, bankruptcy, unemployment or illness to be expressed. Remember that moving house, or becoming separated from a spouse, or losing a limb, or even entering retirement, can also impose deep feelings of bereavement. Acknowledge the depth of Christ's bereavement at the loss of his friend. What does this tell us about Jesus? Group prayer for those suffering bereavement at this time could well highlight some stages that sometimes manifest themselves—shock, anger, guilt, depression, to name only a few. In silent prayer, each stage might be highlighted for attention to bring healing to those present. Promises of Jesus might be read at intervals throughout this prayer time.

- Ask what might trap us in the tombs of our personal lives. Discuss what it might mean to have the courage to risk emerging from these personal 'tombs'. Make space for shared personal stories from group members witnessing to his touch in their past, if such accounts are volunteered.

- Give thanks for our Old Testament roots and the covenants that God made, from Abraham right down to the Lord's new covenant work of salvation through his death and resurrection. Do we see his faithful love from Genesis to Calvary as a rich heritage of our own? Perhaps the group might like to present the line of God's purpose creatively in some visual form. A collage or Christian 'family tree' of some kind could include the main characters in scripture—patriarchs, prophets, kings, faithful servants of Yahweh and later also of Jesus. (This exercise might help some of the members of the group whose talents lie more in the area of visual than verbal communication, enabling everyone to articulate their beliefs.)

- Having studied how God equips us for service, take time to affirm the positive attributes of each individual. Take a long strip of paper for each group member, with his or her name at the top. Pass the strips around and let everyone write a phrase or word to describe the named person's positive attributes, folding it under so that their comment is not seen, before passing it to the next person. When each member takes home the finished strip bearing their name, it acts as a powerful encouragement from the group and reaffirms that person in the knowledge of how God is equipping them in his service.

WEEK FOUR: THE COST

- Discuss how we can show 'extravagant' love for Jesus. Explore what might prevent us from doing so, and discuss the remedy. Is it difficult for some Christians to bring their head and their heart into alignment? Discuss ways to 'unfreeze' the heart when the head already acknowledges Christ intellectually. Perhaps some members might share instances when God 'warmed' their hearts and ignited their spiritual passion for him. Pray together that the group may experience his heartfelt touch this Lent.

- What practical act or sacrificial giving might we undertake either personally, or as a group, to show our love for Jesus this Lenten season? (A new project to help the local community might develop from the suggestions.)

- Discuss each of the Lenten 'objects' from which the traveller had to choose, and share what contemporary lessons can be learnt from them: the casket of nard; the bracken/palm branch; the donkey; the goblet for the Lord's supper; the sword; the thirty pieces of silver; the towel and basin; the crown of thorns.

  (You might arrange, the previous week, for group members to bring along similar physical objects, bought, borrowed or made, to represent each item. Never underestimate the power of a 'visual aid' to inspire discussion with any age group.)

WEEK FIVE: CHOICES

- If we choose to *serve*, what will it cost us in today's society? What is the modern equivalent of 'foot-washing', within family life, within professional life, within the Church?

- If we choose to *obey*, how will it affect our 21st-century lifestyle, or our pride, our finances, our plans for the future, where we live, whom we marry, how we spend our leisure time?

- If we choose to *watch* with him, can we keep our spiritual armour in working order? What changes do we need to make to our life in order to keep the armour in good condition?

- If we choose to enter into a *relationship* with Jesus, can we learn to love him unconditionally, even when his actions in our lives, or his instructions to us, seem to make no sense according to our understanding? What steps can we take to ensure that we do not 'run ahead' of him, causing disaster?

- If we choose the path of *peace*, what personal tools of violence must we surrender? What angry uses of head or heart or tongue must we reject? What forgiveness must we seek—who should we phone tonight?

- If we choose to *lean* only on Christ, refusing to depend on any other strength, weapons or abilities that we might think we possess, are we prepared for the position of vulnerability, the possible suffering that may result? Can we trust his promises? (1 Thessalonians 5:24).

- If we choose to *witness* to what the Lord has done for us, can we take the embarrassment, the scorn, perhaps dangerous consequences in our work, maybe costly reactions at home, or the loneliness of a Peter by the fireside? Or have we ever heard the cock crow twice? God forgave Peter; he can forgive us. Can we forgive ourselves? (A helpful passage for further study would be John 21:15–17.)

- If we choose *truth*, can we stand in contemporary places of power and pain and risk our position, our popularity and our pride to share our vision—as Martin Luther did, as Martin Luther King did, as Mother Teresa did, and *not* as Pilate did? Can we each help the Church to refuse to wash its hands of the responsibility to make judgments for truth in our world?

WEEK SIX: THE FINAL FURLONG

- Your group may appreciate an evening spent with some of the many great compositions of Christian music relating to Holy Week and Easter, during which they can be invited to contemplate the events of this final furlong in silence. End with a time of group prayer in pairs or small cells.

- Other groups might find it beneficial to compose a corporate 'map' of their journey thus far. Give time for each individual to share a lesson learnt if they so desire, while a group member with artistic gifts sketches a symbol on the 'map' to represent what that individual is saying. Display the 'map' on the floor, in the midst of the group, where it can be seen by all. Some individuals may wish not to speak but to draw upon the 'map' themselves in silence.

- Invite each member to imagine that they were literally at the cross. What would they say to Jesus? (Give time for contemplation as instrumental music plays.)

- In contemplation of the cross, slowly repeat the child's prayer that Jesus uttered at his dying: 'Father, into your hands I commit my spirit' (Luke 23:46). As this prayer is echoed again and again by each member of the group, the leader might interject the other phrases spoken by Jesus from the cross and also the affirmation from those who recognized his true nature: 'Truly this man was the Son of God' (Mark 15:39).

- Another exercise of contemplation would be to split the group into smaller 'cells' and allocate a separate name to each one, using the names of the characters whose presence assisted Jesus during those dramatic events: John the beloved disciple; Simon of Cyrene; Mary the mother; Mary the aunt; Mary of Magdala; the repentant thief; the centurion; Joseph of Arimathea; Nicodemus.

After discussion of their character's role in the unfolding events of that week, a spokesperson from each cell might draw their comments and findings together by presenting to the larger group an impromptu short meditation, describing how they 'helped' Jesus on his way to Calvary, speaking in the first person: 'I was there and I saw… I felt… I then… I know… I will always remember… I thank the Lord for… I am assured that…'. Discuss in the group the assurance that the apostle Paul was able to affirm (2 Timothy 1:12).

Note: To look upon Christ on the cross must be to experience our own Calvary unafraid. Your group will bring to the final hours of Christ's Passion many sensations and past experiences. A great number of people look forward to the jubilant music and affirmation associated with Easter Sunday but dread to relive the events of Good Friday. Many shrink from too close a scrutiny of these final hours when Christ hung upon the cross. I have heard folk expressing reasons for avoiding them: 'It's too sad,' they say, 'too depressing, too violent.' These same folk often watch horror films or violent scenes on television, but they know that, when it comes to the story of Christ, the feelings are real.

Why do we cry at sad films? We cry not for the fictional characters upon the screen—we cry for ourselves. The pathos of our own life-events is brought dramatically to our senses as we watch such scenes re-enacted. We must be unafraid to face this reaction, and to allow it to contribute to the healing process that following Christ should initiate in our hearts and minds. The object must be to see Jesus and recognize all that we are, both good and bad.

CELEBRATE THE RISING!

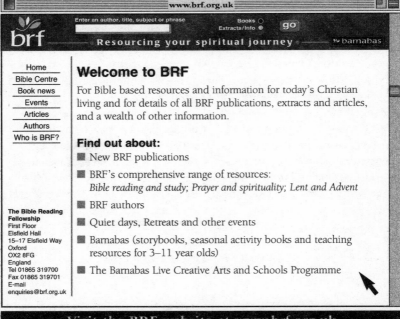

www.brf.org.uk

brf

Enter an author, title, subject or phrase

Books ○
Extracts/Info ●

go

Resourcing your spiritual journey — barnabas

Home
Bible Centre
Book news
Events
Articles
Authors
Who is BRF?

Welcome to BRF

For Bible based resources and information for today's Christian living and for details of all BRF publications, extracts and articles, and a wealth of other information.

Find out about:

▓ New BRF publications

▓ BRF's comprehensive range of resources:
Bible reading and study; Prayer and spirituality; Lent and Advent

▓ BRF authors

▓ Quiet days, Retreats and other events

▓ Barnabas (storybooks, seasonal activity books and teaching resources for 3–11 year olds)

▓ The Barnabas Live Creative Arts and Schools Programme

The Bible Reading Fellowship
First Floor
Elsfield Hall
15–17 Elsfield Way
Oxford
OX2 8FG
England
Tel 01865 319700
Fax 01865 319701
E-mail
enquiries@brf.org.uk

Visit the BRF website at www.brf.org.uk

BRF is a Registered Charity